✿ ✿

Thus, lit and launched, up and up roared and soared
A rocket, till the key o' the vault was reached,
And wide heaven held, a breathless minute-space
In brilliant usurpature: . . .

now decline must be.

✿ THE RING AND THE BOOK

BOYD LITZINGER

TIME'S REVENGES

Browning's Reputation as a Thinker, 1889–1962

THE UNIVERSITY OF TENNESSEE PRESS ❄ KNOXVILLE

FOR

Toni ✿ Michael ✿ Gretchen

CONTENTS

As long as there's no lying, let us have as much Saturday Review-
ing as you like; they're our natural enemies, and I rather enjoy
the practise of "knagging" myself. ⚙ BROWNING ON CRITICS

INTRODUCTION

IT IS A COMMON OBSERVATION THAT
the literary dicta of one period are as often as not rejected
in later times and that poets who please one generation
frequently fail to satisfy the next. Thus Shakespeare has
fared less well in some centuries than in others, and the once
popular poetry of Alfred Austin is now all but forgotten.
The neglect of the great Victorians during the Twenties
and Thirties is another example of critical opinion's
fickleness. Why such reverses occur is always a matter of
interest: causes are sought and often found, and the processes of the shifts themselves are always worth the trouble
of investigation.

Robert Browning's reputation as a thinker is a case in
point. Everyone knows that at one time Browning was
much admired as a philosopher who chose to speak through
verse. Today, as is equally evident, he is not. Critics and
literary historians are aware of a change, but the course
of that change has never been traced with care. That it has
not is surprising because, as we shall see, the images of
Browning the poet and Browning the thinker were fused
almost inseparably in the minds of commentators who
wrote between 1890 and 1920. This gap in Browning
scholarship can be accounted for in part by the very disre-
gard which modern writers show for Browning's thought.
They might justify themselves by arguing that there is no

need to investigate that which no longer exists, but this kind of justification would be specious. Again, there can be no doubt that the close association in many minds between Browning's thought and a Pollyanna optimism (derived, often, from a naive reading of the songs from *Pippa Passes*) serves as another deterrent in an age when optimism is not the popular attitude. Still further there is the reluctance of the modern critic to deal with any poet as a thinker for fear that philosophic and moral considerations will obscure aesthetic judgments. Whatever the reasons, the gap does exist, and one of my purposes here is to close it.

One can hardly understand the impact and influence of Browning's poetry upon the reading public without a sound conception of his reputation as a thinker; to talk about Browning's influence without measuring one of the most important aspects of that influence is to give at best an incomplete report. As well as presenting an overall picture of the poet's reputation for serious thought, this study shows clearly those elements of Browning's poetry which were found worthy of the critics' praise and those which led to his decline from the heights. As it shows the decline in influence of those who promulgated Browning's reputation as a philosopher, it also chronicles the rise and development of the opposition to Browning and his "message." And a picture of changing tastes and critical approaches is inevitably displayed.

The reader will quickly learn that this is neither an essay in literary criticism nor an excursion into philosophy. It is, instead, a form of social history. I have preferred to present facts rather than to comment personally upon them, knowing full well that I have chosen the most modest—perhaps least stimulating—of several tasks open to the student of Browning. I have not read and written without forming personal opinions, but I have restricted my own judgments to the concluding chapter and to a few passages in this introduction. If in the body of the book I have refrained from criticizing an occasional fatuous comment, the reader will be under no similar constraint.

As an aid to those who hope to discern trends in the criticism of Browning's philosophy, the general organization is chronological. Within each chapter, three general groups are distinguished: the critics who are generally favorable toward the poet; those who are generally unfavorable; and those who can most fairly be described as moderate. In each chapter the space devoted to each category is roughly proportional to the importance of the body of criticism under discussion. This inner organization allows a sharp focus on each critical position in a given decade. I have attempted to present each case as fairly and fully as accuracy and clarity require. The weakness of this organization lies in the impression one may get that there have always been sharply separated schools of Browning criticism, or that the various critics have been members of armed camps or opposing armies. It must not be assumed that set battles were fought, with subsequent victories and defeats. There is, indeed, a line of descent from some of the enthusiasts of the Browning Societies to Dallas Kenmare, and from Santayana to Richard Altick, but the line is collateral rather than direct. A few of the critics have, of course, been bellicose, but the history of all Browning criticism has been a matter of action-reaction or, to shift the figure, of critical ebbs and flows.

It ought also to be noted that the materials involved— the individual comments—are marked by peculiarities which tend to complicate the picture of Browning's reputation for serious thought. For example, the various commentators are by no means in agreement in their definitions of *thought* and *thinking:* some use the terms to describe simple mental processes; some mean to imply subtlety of mind; others mean to discuss theology, ethics, or metaphysics; still others merely wish to praise or blame a single "thought" which supports or opposes one of their own. Readers unfamiliar with the history of Browning scholarship may be disappointed to find that the critics have not been treating Browning in the modern manner. Almost without exception, they have dealt with him as a discursive thinker; the work of Erich Auerbach, Ernst Cassirer, Suzanne Langer, and others has had little influence on Browning criticism. This is understandable, if disappointing: Browning's poetic fortunes had sunk to a low level by the time the philosopher-critics who work in terms of symbolic form, presentational thought, myth, and archetype began to exert strong influence in the world of letters. Perhaps future Browning critics will work from more nearly current concepts.

Critical acumen varies among the writers considered here, and few of them, unfortunately, have bolstered their arguments with adequate supporting evidence. It will be seen as well that some interpretations of Browning's thought are poles apart, a matter only confounded the more by the fact that there never has been any solid agreement on the problem of separating Browning's personal from his dramatic utterances. The song from *Pippa Passes* which concludes with "God's in his heaven—/All's right with the world" may serve as an example, for it admits of at least three interpretations: that it embodies the heart of Browning's philosophy; that it represents, at best, an oversimplification of that philosophy; finally, that the philosophy implied in the lines is more Pippa's than Browning's. Instances of contradictory and ambiguous interpretation multiply, inevitably complicating matters and making decisive judgments about any particular point in Browning's creed most difficult.

Each critical comment, either for or against Browning, has a complex significance for this study. Most obviously it reflects the critic's opinion of Browning as a thinker. Next, it exerts a direct influence—however slight, however immeasurable—upon Browning's reputation as a thinker. Third—as in the case of a printed sermon or classroom lecture—it may have exerted an even subtler indirect influence upon that reputation. And last, each criticism represents a small fragment to be fitted into a mosaic that will at last depict Browning's reputation as a thinker.

As I look over the material I have handled, I must say that the adverse critics have, over the decades, had the best of the argument. No one among the favorable critics of the early decades was as effective in argument as John Robertson, George Santayana, or Henry Jones.[1] Robertson was cleverly and pointedly destructive; he obviously enjoyed his iconoclastic attack on Browning's theology, striking through it at an intellectually impoverished generation. Santayana's literary style and philosophical stature lend weight to his severe strictures. Given his initial premise concerning the proper end of philosophy, he is unanswerable. Both Santayana and Robertson, however, suffer somewhat from the excesses of their literary virtues. The voice of neither rises to hysteria, but Robertson's is strident and Santayana's is not marked by that imperturbability one has learned to expect from him.

To my mind, Henry Jones has made the most damaging attack upon Browning the thinker. *Browning as a Philosophical and Religious Teacher* is, on the whole, a sympathetic book. It is not scholarly in the modern sense, but Jones had read Browning very carefully indeed, and the questions he raised concerning Browning's intellectual agnosticism and treatment of the problem of evil are valid ones which have not yet been adequately answered by Browning's supporters.

[1]For discussion of Jones, see pp. 17–21; Santayana, pp. 34–38; Robertson, pp. 38–39.

Among the recent adverse critics, Betty Miller and Richard D. Altick have been effective and, I believe, influential.[2] Mrs. Miller's *Robert Browning: A Portrait* is, in many ways, the best of recent books on Browning. Full as it is of fine insights and sometimes startling judgments, it is essentially a destructive book. Browning the man, the poet, *and* the thinker comes off badly, and one gets the impression that a thesis is ridden too hard. That Shelley and Browning's mother were important influences upon the poet is not to be denied, but to argue that every conflict of mind and thought, desire and fulfillment can be explained in terms of these influences is too simple, too pat. The psychoanalytical approach can sometimes be fruitful, but it is not to every reader's taste. Professor Altick's "The Private Life of Robert Browning" is wittily done, and in it Browning's reputation reaches a very low point; but the argument suffers somewhat from an occasional clever cut which depends upon an oversimplification.

Browning's defenders have been numerous, but few have been effective. Many—like William Lyon Phelps— have written enthusiastic appreciations, and many have professed strong faith in Browning's philosophy, but assertions cannot substitute for rational analysis or reasoned argument. Among recent writers, Professor Kenneth L. Knickerbocker is one of very few who have attempted reasoned defenses.[3] His two essays (one in answer to Santayana, the other in answer to Altick) meet the adverse critics head-on and are argued from a close knowledge of Browning and Browning scholarship. He seems to me to be more effective against Altick than against Santayana, for he is able to seize upon an occasional extreme statement with telling force. The answer to Santayana is more difficult to

[2]For discussion of Altick, see pp. 135–137; Miller, pp. 141–143.
[3]For discussion of Knickerbocker, see pp. 151–153.

evaluate, because it has its roots in a fundamental disagreement over the nature, the aims, and the validity of philosophic systems. By denying Santayana's premises, Knickerbocker can argue that Santayana was temperamentally incapable of judging Browning fairly. But these essays are directed against specific schools of adverse criticism, and they do not allow space for positive evaluations of Browning as a thinker.

Whatever the present state of the question, it seems certain that commentary will continue. As in the past, so in the future; the patient reader will, with Chaucer, remark: "Diverse folk diversely they seyde."

Yes, the British Public like, and more than like me, this week,
they let their admiration ray out on me.

❀ BROWNING TO JULIA WEDGWOOD

ALL'S RIGHT WITH THE WORLD

WHEN BROWNING DIED PEACEFULLY in Venice on December 12, 1889, his fame as a poet and as a serious thinker was established. Recognition had been slow in coming to him, but it came within his lifetime; and with it came a reputation for serious, helpful, and valid thought. In many quarters, Browning was praised as a philosopher in verse. From almost the very beginning of his poetic career the critics had seen in his poetry certain intellectual qualities which, given nurture, were to lead to the philosophizing of *La Saisiaz* and *Ferishtah's Fancies*. For example, in 1833 an anonymous reviewer remarked in *The Atlas* that *Pauline* was "metaphysical throughout, or intended to be so."[1] Two years later, John Forster, one of Browning's earliest admirers, praised the intellectual powers displayed in *Paracelsus;*[2] and, after the failure of *Sordello* had been outlived, the poet slowly gained for himself a reputation as a thinker.

When in 1881 the indefatigable Furnivall founded the Browning Society, evangelical promotion of Browning as a thinker was begun in earnest. That Browning's supporters were successful in their activities no one who has read something of the ensuing chorus of praise in both England and America can possibly doubt. Many papers published by the Society bore such titles as "Browning's Philosophy," "On

[1] *The Atlas* (April 14, 1833), p. 28.
[2] *The Examiner* (September 6, 1835), pp. 563–565.

1

Browning as a Teacher of the Nineteenth Century," and "Browning's Poems on God and Immortality as Bearing on His Life Here." As the compilers of the latest Browning bibliography comment, the introductory address delivered to the first meeting of the Browning Society "bore heavily on Browning as a religious leader, setting a keynote for much of the Society's later activity."[3]

Browning's death in 1889, therefore, served merely as a convenient impetus to the various societies and to his numerous following to spread his philosophy and fame to the ends of the earth. The resultant flood of publications on Browning during the first few years following his death was so great that the bibliographers have never made an attempt to list them all, and it may be stated with confidence that the poet's reputation as a thinker was at its highest during these years.

Thus it is not unexpected that the favorable criticism of Browning as a thinker bulks very large during the years 1889–1899; nor is it surprising that there was wide disagreement among the critics over such matters as what Browning's message was, what he had to say about any particular subject, whether the poet ought to be sacrificed to the philosopher, and whether the activities of the societies did more good or harm to the poet's reputation among the masses. In one thing, however, they were agreed: Browning was a thinker.

One or two printed comments, culled from literally hundreds like them, will indicate the esteem in which Browning the thinker was held. Hamilton Wright Mabie wrote in 1892 that "No other [English poet] has so completely mastered the larger movement of modern thought on the constructive side, or so deeply felt and so adequately interpreted the modern spirit."[4] F. Mary Wilson, introducing the readers of 1891 to

[3]Leslie N. Broughton, Clark S. Northup, and Robert Pearsall, *Robert Browning: A Bibliography, 1830–1950* (Ithaca, 1953), p. 133.

[4]"Robert Browning," *Essays in Literary Interpretation* (New York, 1892), pp. 103–104, 110.

Browning's poetry, wrote: "Browning is not solely a poetic
artist, he is besides that a 'thinker,' with so persistent an answer to the ultimate question of life that few of his poems
can be appraised without reference to it."[5] And John Jay
Chapman challenged those who would refuse Browning the
thinker's crown by writing, "We need not apologize for treating Browning as a theologian and a doctor of philosophy, for
he spent a long life in trying to show that a poet is always really
both—and he has almost convinced us."[6]

A study of the criticism of this period leads to the conclusion that Browning was admired chiefly, though not exclusively, for two reasons. First, many thought him the defender
of Christianity, though interpretations of Browning's Christian
"teachings" vary widely enough to cover the whole range of
Protestant thought. This divergence of views on Browning's
Christianity constitutes, in fact, a matter which should be of
interest to the historian of society and religion. Second, many
admired him as the chief proponent of an optimistic *Weltansicht* which reflected their own highest aspirations. Growing
out of these two views of Browning, and in a sense encom-
passing both, a third role developed: that of Browning the
philosopher-prophet. But this role is an effect rather than a
cause and is for the present less important than an examination of the praise accorded Browning the Defender of Christianity and Browning the Optimist between 1889 and the
close of the century.

Writing for *The Atlantic Monthly* in 1890, an anonymous
author attempted to assess Browning's influence as a religious
teacher by emphasizing the effectiveness of his "simplification
of religion." He concluded that

> Browning ... owes no small part of his real influence and

[5]*A Primer on Browning* (London, 1891), p. 17.
[6]"Robert Browning," *Emerson and Other Essays* (New York, 1898),
p. 188.

nearness to many lives to this fervent belief in the voice and
the light within, the intuition of the soul, the piety of the
simple reverence and trust, the faith in the "one divine event"
of all. Outside of the church this preaching has been a com-
pensation for professed religion, and within it a strengthening
and vivifying energy.[7]

This is a penetrating observation. To many, Browning's religious appeal was strong because of its apparent simplicity.
To the reader who goes no further than *Saul, Rabbi Ben
Ezra, A Death in the Desert,* and *Christmas-Eve*—and there
were many who went little further—Browning's preference
for simple faith is plain. Besides, was it not evident from *A
Death in the Desert* and *Christmas-Eve* that Browning stood
firm against the perplexing and disturbing "historical" critics
of the Bible? Was he not reared in a healthy atmosphere
of Nonconformity? Finally, did he not unmask in many a
poem—e.g., *Bishop Blougram's Apology, The Confessional,*
and *Holy-Cross Day*—those notorious followers of Antichrist,
the papists? These were all sound recommendations to many
a reader of Browning's poems.

Among these readers was Clara Bloomfield-Moore, a close
friend of Browning in his later years, who wrote in 1890:

All who are in full sympathy with the poet in his views . . .
feel no doubt that he expounds the gospel after the teachings
of our Holy Master, rather than after the teachings of the
Jewish high-priests. . . . Such are the teachings that we find
on every page of Browning's most profound poems; and the
poet lived up to his teachings in full measure of faith and of
loyalty.[8]

This same appeal to a religion based upon simplicity and
Scripture alone was matter for comment during the same year

[7]"Robert Browning," *The Atlantic Monthly,* LXV (1890), 245.
[8]"Robert Browning," *Lippincott's Magazine,* XLV (1890), 687.

by Moncure D. Conway and an anonymous contributor to *Living Age*. The latter made the point that the views Browning expressed in his poetry stemmed from his Protestant upbringing, and exulted over Browning's "unfaltering witness to the faith of his youth."[9] Conway, more cautious, explained that although Browning was sympathetic with all shades of religious convictions, "His picture in 'Christmas Eve' of the philosopher in the wretched conventicle with the vulgar worshippers . . . choosing, nevertheless, to fix his place there, has much truth in it."[10]

Other aspects of Browning's religious teachings were discussed during the first years of the decade by Anna Swanwick, Stopford Brooke, Mary Wilson, and H. E. Shepherd, and the obvious differences among their points of view make only the more interesting the fact that all could praise alike and with nearly equal fervor the poet's religious position. Anna Swanwick noted the "witness borne by Robert Browning to the fundamental truths of religion," truths which included a conception of man "as a twofold being, allied to God by his spiritual nature, destined accordingly to endless progress, and haunted forever by visions of perfection transcending his experience."[11] Brooke's interpretation of Browning's religious appeal is different. It was his belief that Browning somehow got to the roots of man's belief and that his poetry represented "a wholly new turn in theology—which went below dogma to the impassioned human desires out of which dogma had grown."[12] Without disclosing just how dogma grew out of "impassioned human desires" or how Browning made this point valid, Brooke went on to couple Browning and Tennyson in praise: "Both maintain for us the mighty

[9]"Robert Browning," *Living Age*, CLXXXVI (1890), 783–784.
[10]"Recollections of Robert Browning," *Nation*, L (1890), 28.
[11]*Poets the Interpreters of Their Age* (London, 1892), p. 387.
[12]"Robert Browning," *The Contemporary Review*, LVII (1890), 142.

truths of God's fatherhood and man's perfection beyond death."[13]

Both Shepherd and Mrs. Wilson took still a different point of view, recognizing Browning as part of the religious turmoil of his age. Although the former was concerned primarily with a study of Browning's use of language, he first of all acknowledged the poet's right to the title "subtlest assertor of the soul in song" and proclaimed that "The deep and obstinate questionings of invisible things are portrayed [by Browning] as by no other hand."[14] Mrs. Wilson wrote of him:

> If he did not originate the broadest expression of nineteenth century belief, at least he transmutes it, so that through his poetry it re-enters many a soul with healing in its wings. To many people his words are a later evangel of reasonable Christianity.[15]

This same service of interpreting religion to his century was attributed to Browning from time to time throughout the remainder of the decade. Edward Berdoe, writing in 1895, said that Browning "taught us a pure religion reasonable and manly, robust and in harmony with the science of the age, and few would listen and fewer still would heed. Yet the age had such need of him!"[16] Similarly, James Mudge wrote that Browning "stated the old truths of Christianity in the language of the nineteenth century, . . . ever teaching the world dauntless courage, sublime faith, and deathless love."[17] It was Mudge, too, who attempted to show that Browning's religion was tainted by none of the pseudo-intellectualism of his time, for he claimed that a careful reader will search

[13]*Ibid.,* p. 152.
[14]"Robert Browning," *MLN,* V (1890), 36.
[15]Wilson, pp. 17–18.
[16]*Browning Studies* (New York, 1895), p. vi.
[17]"The Poetry, Personality, and Potency of Robert Browning," *Methodist Review,* CLII (1898), 648.

Browning's utterances in vain for such despicable attitudes as "mere naturalism," agnosticism, or "cold, colorless, humanitarianism."[18] In short, whereas Berdoe regarded Browning as the interpreter of the best in the "reasonable" and "scientific" religion of the later nineteenth century, Mudge praised him for refusing to water down his Christianity by adjusting it to the times.

Here also should be noted the favorable comments of John Jay Chapman in 1898 and Vida Scudder in 1895, for both writers made much of Browning's optimistic faith. Miss Scudder, in fact, gave him a place of prime importance chiefly because of his basically Christian outlook. She wrote:

> . . . it is in Browning that Christianity finds its most joyous and undaunted exponent. From "Paracelsus" to "Ferishtah's Fancies" and "Asolando," a definite and devout Christianity shows through his work. No important poem is untouched by it, except when deliberately and for specific purposes excluded; and in the greatest poems, it is assumed supreme.[19]

So strongly grounded was this religious position, she continued, that Browning was able to face confidently all problems, doubts, and questionings. "If now and again a world-old puzzle refuses to yield," she wrote, "the poet hastens serenely around it, and finds faith waiting on the other side."[20] And the overall admiring tone of her remarks proves that Miss Scudder was not making light of Browning's easy avoidance of these "world-old puzzles." Chapman's comments are to the same effect:

> Religion was at the basis of his character. . . . It was inevitable that Robert Browning should find and seize upon as his own

[18]*Ibid.*, p. 165.

[19]Vida D. Scudder, *The Life of the Spirit in the Modern English Poets* (Boston, 1895), p. 334.

[20]*Ibid.*, p. 335.

all that was optimistic in Christian theology. Everything that was hopeful his spirit accepted; . . . what was distressing he rejected or explained away. In the world of Robert Browning *everything* was right.[21]

A suitable finishing touch on this portrait of Browning as a religious teacher was supplied by Augustus H. Strong, author of *The Great Poets and Their Theology:*

> I am inclined to commend the reading of Robert Browning to all preachers and theologians, as well as to all thoughtful Christian people. He is the most learned, stirring, impressive literary teacher of our time—but he is a religious philosopher as well. . . . He who would serve men's highest interests as secular or religious teachers, will find more of illustration, more of stimulus, in Browning than in any other writer.[22]

Aside from the poet's religious message and its inspirational value, his much-talked-about optimism proved in the 1890's to be the characteristic most highly regarded by those who admired Browning as a thinker. His robust religiousness served them as a spiritual tonic, and his optimism was equally useful as a moral stimulant. For most of these favorable critics, however, Browning's optimism was more than a happy outlook on life. It was a full-hearted acceptance of life, a joyful call to live life to the fullest, to satisfy the whole man by energetic activity both of body and of soul. Asceticism and denial of self played no part in this interpretation, and the cry of "Fight ever—there as here!" shouted on the last page of the *Asolando* volume echoed and re-echoed for a decade in the writing of many of Browning's disciples.

Perhaps this view of Browning's optimism, based in considerable measure upon the physical and emotional faculties, was best explained by Arthur Waugh, who wrote in 1890:

[21]Chapman, pp. 187–188.
[22](Philadelphia, 1897), pp. 396–397.

... what could be simpler than the direct theme of almost all Browning's poetry... ? The life which we know was, as he saw it, a preparation for some further, fuller existence, in which ... every unfulfilled impulse would burst into fruition. Life, then, must be concentrated upon the emotions; every enthusiasm must be given play, but the play of all must be subordinated by a sense of the impossibility of realizing the true power of the faculties in this life.[23]

The emphasis upon the emotions, upon the releasing of restraints, together with a resulting exhilaration, seems to have played a large part in the praise of Browning's optimism. A writer in *The Atlantic Monthly* remarked in 1890 that "The energy of action in Browning's work has also counted for much in the appeal to his contemporaries,"[24] and Amy Sharp, who wrote to introduce Browning to university extension students, explained in 1891 that since he considered this world "a preparation for 'more life and fuller' beyond the veil," he "does not place his ideal in disciplined obedience and law and duty; but in disciplined *activity*, continuous aspiration from height to height."[25] Continuing in this vein she declared further that the poet "denounces the man or woman who stifles an arousing impulse in obedience to prudential motives."[26] These early favorable commentaries on optimism show how easily Browning has become the antithesis of Carlyle, with his gloomy outlook and his insistence upon blind obedience to the Great God Work. Browning, with his own insistence upon fulfillment of one's self through impulsive action, seems to have been welcomed as the bearer of a needed panacea.

The middle years of this decade found the praise of Browning's optimism still blooming. Dean Farrar, commemorating the seventh anniversary of Browning's death, gave, as it were,

[23]*Robert Browning* (London, 1890), pp. 143–144.
[24]"Robert Browning," p. 246.
[25]"Robert Browning," *Victorian Poets* (London, 1891), pp. 44–45.
[26]*Ibid.,* p. 47.

an ecclesiastical sanction to this energetic optimism, although he did not stress as heavily as did many during this decade the requisite freedom from restraint. Calling Browning's optimism "so needful a lesson to an age so sick as ours is with despondency and doubt," Dean Farrar claimed that Browning's is an optimism

> ... large-sighted and nobly masculine. It is based on his view of man, and of the life of man, its unity, its immortality, its progress even through failures and defects. ... It is the optimism of a man who "saw life steadily and saw it whole."[27]

A similar defense of Browning's optimism as a well-considered plan of life was that published in *The Dial* in 1895 over the initials W. N. G., who sought to differentiate between the poet's optimism and the shallow, Pollyanna variety. Wrote W. N. G.:

> There is all the difference in the world between an optimism that is the result of ignorance and inexperience—an optimism that is not at all disagreeable in a football champion or a robust school-graduate—and an optimism like St. Paul's and like Browning's, which differs from frank pessimism only in its superb assumption of a yet unseen and incomprehensible hereafter and beyond: "On the earth the broken arch: in the heavens the perfect round." [*sic*][28]

Two years later, Augustine Birrell made the same point in his defense of the poet's optimism,[29] and F. Herbert Stead wrote

[27]"The Significance of Browning's Message," *Review of Reviews,* XV (1897), 188.

[28]"Browning's Optimism, So-Called," *The Dial,* XVIII (1895), 290.

[29]"Robert Browning: An Address Delivered at the Browning Hall Settlement, December 12, 1897," *The Collected Essays and Addresses of the Rt. Hon. Augustine Birrell, 1880–1920* (London, 1922), II, 136.

that "Only the optimism of Browning does justice to . . . [the English people's] expansive and exuberant energies."[30]

The last two years of the century saw more praise heaped upon Browning for the same reason. For example, James Mudge (1898) attributed much of Browning's influence to his optimistic preachments,[31] and finally, in 1899, William Ralph Inge praised the happy conjunction of religion and optimism in Browning's poetry. This optimism, he wrote, this "trust in real success through apparent disappointments —a trust even *based* on the consciousness of present failure—is certainly one of the noblest parts of his religious philosophy."[32]

Taking positions at various points between the critics who hold a generally favorable view of Browning as a thinker and those who do not are a number of commentators who can best be described as moderates. All of them recognize in one way or another Browning's reputation for serious thought, but none of them give their wholehearted approval to it. Some of them explain without judging the poet's ideas or his message, some seem to advise moderation in discussing the subject, and still others find room for both praise and blame in estimating Browning's philosophy of life.

The range of "explainers" is wide. For example, Mrs. Sutherland Orr in 1891, George Saintsbury in 1896, and Clement K. Shorter in 1897 all had comments to make about Browning's religious thought, but none of these made judgments for the readers. Both Mrs. Orr and Saintsbury recognized the poet's unorthodoxy. To Saintsbury the fact was of no great import: "If he was not exactly what is commonly

[30]"Browning as a Poet of the Plain People," *Review of Reviews,* XV (1897), 192.

[31]Mudge, p. 651.

[32]William Ralph Inge, *Christian Mysticism Considered in Eight Lectures Before the University of Oxford* (London, 1899), p. 320.

called orthodox in religion, and if his philosophy was of a distinctly vague order, he was always 'on the side of the angels' in theology, in metaphysics, in ethics."[33] On the other hand the critic deplored "handbooks solemnly addressed to neophytes in Browningism, as if the cult were a science or art."[34] Mrs. Orr was pretty much in agreement with Saintsbury, at least in her article on "The Religious Opinions of Robert Browning." She judged the poet not "Christian in the orthodox sense of the word" because he denied damnation, any belief in revelation, and usual conceptions of God and the hereafter.[35] On the other hand, she found him a firm believer in Christ as a manifestation of God's love, if not as the Redeemer,[36] and traced his religious beliefs to his Nonconformist rearing, saying that "the Evangelical Christian was allied in him to the subjective idealist."[37] Shorter found the same influence working on Browning's thought and poetry when he wrote that "Browning's early Nonconformity, his attendance on the ministrations of an Independent minister gave the ring of the pulpit to every line he wrote."[38]

There is another group of moderate writers whose comments are of interest, for they attempted during the 1890's to shift the emphasis away from Browning as a philosopher while maintaining that what he had to say as a poet was worth listening to. John Nettleship's "On Erroneous Study of Browning" (1890) warned readers of the dramatic quality of Browning's verse and advised them not to read a great deal of philosophy into it.[39] Writing of the philosophical interpreters of Browning

[33]*A History of Nineteenth Century Literature* (*1780–1895*) (New York, 1896), pp. 274–275.

[34]*Ibid.,* p. 273.

[35]Mrs. Sutherland Orr, "The Religious Opinions of Robert Browning, *Contemporary Review,* LX (1891), 878 ff.

[36]*Ibid.,* p. 878.

[37]*Ibid.,* p. 887.

[38]"Victorian Literature," *The Bookman,* V (1897), 480.

[39]John T. Nettleship, *Robert Browning: Essays and Thoughts,* 2nd ed. (London, 1890), p. 337.

he declared, "All such attempts by conscientious students of Browning to read the writer's own theological or other views into poems dealing with portrait drama true, should be gibbeted as high as Haman; they are poisoning the wells."[40] In contrast, Nettleship indicated that he considered Browning a latter-day prophet and teacher, arguing that the poetic message would be of religious and philosophical import even in years to come.[41]

Josiah Royce made clearer this distinction between the philosopher and the dramatic moral teacher. Insisting that Browning is primarily a poet and secondarily a thinker, he explained that Browning's God is a Being whose characteristics are power and love[42] and that Browning's love is the overcoming of adversity. "If these things are so," continued Royce, "then even the divine love itself must need for its fulfilment these struggles, ... failures, ... sins, hopes, and horrors of the world of human passion in which, according to our poet, the divine is incarnate."[43] Again, however, he made his distinction that this conclusion of Browning's is an intuition supported by experience, but never a philosophy.[44] Stopford Brooke, in a private letter, said the same thing even more strongly:

> As to calling him a "thinker," I never did it. I called him a Poet, who is as much above a thinker as a man is above an oyster. Thinkers bore me; for they are so fond of thinking that they think; and the Thinker alone is nowhere and no good in the Universe. He just suits this little scrap of a planet with all its half existences struggling, while they are here, towards life.[45]

[40]*Ibid.*, p. 338.
[41]*Ibid.*, p. 454.
[42]Josiah Royce, "Browning's Theism," *Boston Browning Society Papers* (New York, 1897; hereafter cited as *BBSP*), pp. 18–25.
[43]*Ibid.*, p. 33.
[44]*Ibid.*, p. 34.
[45]Quoted in Lawrence P. Jacks, *The Life and Letters of Stopford A. Brooke* (New York, 1917), II, 538.

The point of moderation is evident. Browning does not receive praise as a thinker from these writers, but what of that? The poet is infinitely superior anyway.

Compared with the favorable criticism between 1889 and 1899 the adverse comments about Browning as a thinker were few. None of these critics went about their work with the gusto some of their successors would display. With a few exceptions, the unfavorable comments were sniping attacks, not full-faced assaults on Browning's thought.

Some writers who registered unfavorable remarks about the lack of depth in Browning's thought connected the fault with the poet's obscurity, supposed or real. Early in 1890, for instance, Robert Niven put the blame for Browning's obscurity on the poet's inability to make his ideas intelligible. To those who would claim that Browning's thought was too deep, too great for clear expression, Niven said:

> Can the impartial critic of Browning's poems entertain this plea? Not so. . . . The impartial critic has to go further, and to say not merely that Browning's thought is not of that high, rare, and original kind supposed, but that he may even be blamed in that, with a message to his fellows less weighty than those of Wordsworth, Carlyle, and Emerson, he outdoes them all in obscurity.[46]

Writing for *Modern Language Notes* in the same year, G. R. McElroy insisted flatly that Browning's obscurity is real and that the poet cannot express himself. "There are things in him," wrote McElroy, "that 'no fellow can find out.' . . . Is he like the average Sophomore, with one thing in his mind and another on his paper?"[47] The line of this argument is then extended to include those who defend Browning by saying

[46]"Browning's Obscurity," *The New England Magazine*, N. S. I (1890), 581.

[47]"And Which, But Who,—Browning's Obscurity," *MLN*, V (1890), 91.

that one cannot expect absolute clarity from the race of prophets, for their thoughts are beyond the grasp of less gifted mortals:

> "The poet-seer" is the high priest of all these mysteries, entering the holy of holies, where we may not follow him, but coming out again with a divine message for the people, God's peace and benediction, not a more tangled puzzle than was before us when we knelt humbly at the shrine, seeking light and guidance. This office of seeing and revealing has been the function of every poet since Homer.... Has this been Mr. Browning's office? I trow not.[48]

Like McElroy and Niven, George Saintsbury linked Browning's profundity with his reputation for obscurity when he wrote in 1895: "The depth of Mr. Browning's thought belongs to the same tradition as his obscurity, and reminds me of those inky pools in the limestone district which look and are reputed to be bottomless till somebody tries them and finds them to be about nineteen foot two."[49]

Some of the adverse critics found flaws in the poet's optimism. These comments are especially interesting, for they betray the fact that most of these critics would have been displeased with whatever conclusions anyone had ever reached about optimism. Certainly none of these were satisfied with Browning's conclusions. A. J. George explained in 1895, for example, that Browning the poet is an optimist, but that Browning the philosopher is not. It is, he wrote, Browning the poet who offers man an optimistic faith. The philosopher is mistaken in not doing so.[50] Joshua Kendall in 1892 found this optimism absent not so much from Browning the philosopher as from Browning the philosopher-in-his-old-age; he believed

---

[48]*Ibid.*

[49]"Browning," *Corrected Impressions* (New York, 1895), p. 110.

[50]A. J. George, "The Optimism of Wordsworth and Browning, in Relation to Modern Philosophy," *BBSP,* pp. 326–328.

that despondency marks the later poems.[51] Saintsbury called
Browning's philosophy "a theory of living and doing more optimist than Carlylism and less fantastic than Ruskinism, but
as vague and as unpractical as either."[52] And Thomas Hardy,
shaking his head perplexedly in the last year of the century,
wrote to his friend Edmund Gosse:

> The longer I live the more does Browning's character seem
> the literary puzzle of the nineteenth century. How could smug
> Christian optimism worthy of a dissenting grocer find a place
> inside a man who was so vast a seer and feeler when on neu-
> tral ground? . . . One day I had a theory which you will call
> horrible—that perceiving he would obtain in a stupid nation
> no hearing as a poet if he gave himself in his entirety, he
> professed a certain mass of commonplace opinion as a bait
> to get the rest of him taken.[53]

On the other hand, as if to show how fruitless are the attempts
of one man to satisfy all minds, we find A. Taylor Innes'
comments on *La Saisiaz* in 1896. Innes was unhappy that
Browning failed in the poem to reach a more optimistic conclusion. Allowing for the poet's depression over the death of
his friend and the limitations of poetry, Innes insisted that
Browning's two assumptions—God and Soul—were equipment sufficient for the job of sustaining optimism in *La
Saisiaz*.[54]

Two critics—Francis Thompson and an unnamed writer
for *The Nation*—objected in the 1889–1899 period to Browning's reputation as a moral teacher, a man with a message to
deliver. It was Thompson's view that Browning is almost en-

[51]"Apparent Failure, In Reality, Ultimate and Substantial Triumph," *BBSP*, p. 125.
[52]Saintsbury, "Browning," pp. 113–114.
[53]Quoted in Carl J. Weber, *Hardy of Wessex, His Life and Literary
Career* (New York, 1940), p. 190.
[54]"La Saisiaz in 1895," *The Contemporary Review*, LXX (1896),
273.

tirely dramatic and that to impute sermonizing to him is to do him an injustice. Finding Browning an objective questioner who came to no conclusions—at least to none he wished to pass on to his readers—Thompson declared himself "unable to find that Browning had, or thought himself to have, any message."[55] In contrast to Thompson, the writer for *The Nation* believed that Browning did have a moral message, but one which was faulty. Writing about those poems of Browning's which are "special pleadings," he concluded that the poet leads his readers to think that "Who understands all, forgives all," a doctrine whose end "is to efface moral judgment and to substitute for it intellectual comprehension ; and usually this results in a practical fatalism, acquiesced in if not actively held."[56] The moral of *The Statue and the Bust* he judged shaky, and the poet's belief that the soul grows through activity, even though the activity may be wrong, he believed opposed by the "noblest thinkers and purest artists," who will not "believe that the doing of evil is to be urged in the interest of true manliness."[57]

This decade's most serious attack against Browning the philosopher was mounted by Henry Jones. His *Browning as a Philosophical and Religious Teacher* (1891) has been much admired as a thorough examination of Browning's thought. Jones was in no way unfriendly to Browning insofar as he is an optimistic man and poet. It is clear, however, that Jones shared no belief that Browning was a philosopher in verse. Pushing aside possible objections that it is unfair to examine Browning's thought as though the poet were a philosopher, Jones held that the poet himself "led the way towards a philosophical interpretation of his work. For he not seldom crossed the line that divides the poet from the philosopher, and all

[55]*Literary Criticisms by Francis Thompson,* ed. by Terence L. Connolly, S. J. (New York, 1948), p. 153.
[56]"Robert Browning," *The Nation,* XLIX (1889), 493.
[57]*Ibid.*

but broke through the strict limits of art in the effort to express—and we might even say to preach—his own idealistic faith."[58] And, he wrote, the poet gave up his right to be judged under the rules of "the intuitive method of art" by trying in his later poems "to meet the difficulties of speculative ethics."[59]

The first matter of importance in Browning's philosophy Jones examined was the poet's optimism. In this, Jones found Browning worthy of praise, but not as a thinker. With Browning, he wrote, this optimism is held as a matter of feeling: "It is not by means of logical demonstration that he helps us to meet the despair of Carlyle. . . . Browning's proofs are the least convincing when he is most aware of his philosophical presuppositions."[60] But since Browning employed his optimism as though it were a philosophy, Jones continued, "many who are distrustful of the systems of the schools, and who are 'neither able to find a faith or to do without one,' may use his optimism as such."[61]

The fallacy in Browning's optimism Jones discovered in its connection with Browning's theory of man's inability to achieve certitude. Browning's optimism is assured, this critic wrote, by his belief that God is the All-Loving; this belief, however, Browning is able to keep up only by casting doubt upon man's knowledge. "Thus," Jones said,

> his optimism and faith in God is finally based upon ignorance. If, on the side of love, he insists . . . on God's communication of His own substance to man; on the side of knowledge he may be called an agnostic, in spite of stray expressions which break through his deliberate theory.[62]

[58]*Browning as a Philosophical and Religious Teacher* (Glasgow, 1891), p. viii.
[59]*Ibid.*, p. 104.
[60]*Ibid.*, p. 90.
[61]*Ibid.*, pp. 91–92.
[62]*Ibid.*, pp. 235–236.

Jones saw a fallacy in Browning's utter rejection of the validity of human knowledge—his belief that the intellect is totally unable to arrive at truth—which

> leads directly into absolute scepticism. And *absolute* scepticism is easily shown to be contradictory. For a theory of nescience, in condemning all knowledge and the faculty of knowledge, condemns itself. If nothing is true, or if nothing is known, then this theory itself is not true, or its truth cannot be known. And if this theory is true, then nothing is true; for this theory, like all others, is the product of a defective intelligence. In whatsoever way the matter is put, there is left no standing ground for the human critic who condemns thought. ... There is this one presupposition which everyone must make, if he is to propound any doctrine whatsoever, even if that doctrine be that no doctrine can be valid; it is the presupposition that knowledge is possible, and that truth can be known. ... It is the starting-point and criterion of all knowledge.[63]

Asking rhetorically why Browning himself failed to see this flat and irreconcilable contradiction, Jones gave two reasons: first, that Browning probably never examined it critically; secondly, that Browning was no metaphysician at all.[64]

The same contradiction over knowledge crops up again in Browning's belief that evil is only apparent or temporary. If Browning felt that a sure knowledge of good and evil would destroy free choice, he solved his difficulty by reducing the facts he did not want to recognize "into phenomena, in the sense of phantoms begotten by the human intellect upon unknown and unknowable realities."[65] And Jones would deny even that such a belief could make for sound morality, thus casting aspersions upon Browning as a moral teacher:

[63]*Ibid.*, pp. 241–242.
[64]*Ibid.*, pp. 242–243.
[65]*Ibid.*, p. 248.

But it was a profound error, which contained in it the destruction of morality and religion, as well as of knowledge,
to make "the quality of God" a love that excludes reason,
and the quality of man an intellect incapable of knowing
truth. . . . A love that was mere emotion could not yield a
motive for morality, or a principle of religion. A philosophy
of life which is based upon agnosticism is an explicit self-
contradiction, which can help no one. We must appeal from
Browning the philosopher to Browning the poet.[66]

Jones therefore must conclude that Browning is at best a
dubious ally even to Christianity, because "In degrading human knowledge, the poet was disloyal to the fundamental
principle of the Christian faith which he professed—that God
can and does manifest himself in man."[67]

Although other criticisms of Browning's philosophy will be
found to be wittier, more scathing, or more scornful, Jones,
as far as he went, was no less effective than any of them. He
covered his chosen ground carefully and without animosity,
thus showing himself to be a friend of the poet but not of the
would-be philosopher.

Despite the adverse comments by Jones and less telling
critics, Browning's reputation as a thinker was quite high
during the decade immediately following his death. Religion
and optimism were the two aspects of his thought most often
found worthy of praise, although the favorable critics had a
good bit to say about many other matters. As a result, the
favorable critics were prone to ignore or to give a back seat
to the poetry of Browning's later years, poetry in which optimism and religious assurance are less marked than in the
poetry of the early and middle periods. The later poems,
which disclose Browning's increasing distrust of human knowledge and the intellect, the adverse critics seized upon for their
evidence; and sometimes, as in the case of Jones, they distin-

[66]*Ibid.*, p. 341.
[67]*Ibid.*, p. 250.

guished the poet—the early Browning—from the philosopher
—the later Browning. His admirers were less willing to admit
this severance of personalities within Browning and were
likely to treat *A Death in the Desert* as though it were as philosophical in method and intent as *La Saisiaz* and the *Parleyings*. In any case, the adverse critics were small in number
and weak in voice, taken as a whole, and the ripples of dissent hardly disturbed the high tide of praise in the 1890's for
Browning the thinker.

I think you are hard on the Society,—not on the vagaries of the gnostic papers—those marked by the "overknowingness" you animadvert upon most justly. ⊙ BROWNING TO J. T. NETTLESHIP

A CRACK SOMEWHERE

LEST THE NEWLY BORN TWENTIETH century should fail in its youthful impiety to recognize the philosophical accomplishments of the Victorian Era, William Pierson Merrill imparted a primer lesson in Tennyson and Browning, two poets who mirrored many of the philosophic aspirations of the nineteenth century. "Each is a great thinker," wrote Merrill,

> who has consecrated the best of his life to the bringing together of the scientific conception of God made necessary by the marvellous discoveries of this century, and the personal or spiritual conception of God made necessary by the demands of man's moral and spiritual life . . . Their keynote is human nature as the interpretation of the divine nature. They are the great teachers of the higher, or spiritual anthropomorphism.[1]

In that statement Merrill implied the problem faced by the preceding generation, the problem stated in many terms—perfect God, imperfect world; good, evil; science, religion; reason, emotion; culture, anarchy—and yet in all its terms seemingly soluble only by the method described by Samuel Johnson as *"discordia concors,"* paradox.[2]

If paradox was to supply the solution to the problem of life, we can readily see why the Victorians turned to their

[1] *Faith and Sight* (New York, 1900), pp. 128–129.
[2] *The Life of Cowley* (1779).

poets for their answers; for had not Wordsworth called the poet "a man . . . endowed with a more lively sensibility, more enthusiasm and tenderness, who has a greater knowledge of human nature, and a more comprehensive soul than are supposed to be common among mankind"? And paradox requires the "comprehensive soul," the ability to see relationships and likenesses where others see them not.

Merrill had no doubt that Robert Browning saw those relationships and had an answer to present to the modern mind. This answer, according to Merrill, involves a system in which God is interpreted in terms of man's spiritual aspirations carried to perfection. As Merrill put it,

> Browning is luminous with the thought that, though God is unknowable, He must be interpreted in some way, and that the best and truest way is through a spiritual anthropomorphism. "I have a right to interpret the infinite as like my best self," is the keynote of his deepest thinking and writing.[3]

Merrill believed that this attitude is to be seen in the *Epilogue* to *Dramatis Personae*, in *Ferishtah's Fancies*, in *Saul*, and in *A Death in the Desert*, but at its clearest and deepest in *Christmas-Eve*, in which Browning achieved a reconciliation between "the Agnostic mind and the craving heart."[4] In this work the poet, examining three approaches to the God-Man relationship, achieved a synthesis by finding that the attempt at an approach is present in all three and that the attempt is more important than the method involved.[5] It will be noted, of course, that this interpretation of *Christmas-Eve* would make that poem another expression of Browning's belief that the struggle is more important than victory.

That this particular solution is both valid and important

[3]Merrill, pp. 137–138.
[4]*Ibid.*, p. 142.
[5]*Ibid.*, p. 143.

is emphasized by Merrill's admonition to the twentieth century that "A profound study of 'Christmas Eve' would prepare the student to grapple with the problems of present-day thought far more fully than would the study of many systems of theology."[6]

Merrill was not the only author to expound Browning's thought with enthusiasm during the early years of the century. Dorothea Beale's *Literary Studies of Poems, New and Old,* published in 1902, contains two essays concerned primarily with Browning as a religious teacher. In one, the author was willing to admit room for disagreement over whether or not Browning was a poet, although she was quite positive that "he is *certainly* a seer."[7] In the second of her studies, Mrs. Beale's enthusiasm waxed almost lyrical. She found that although Browning's philosophy was marked with superficial flaws it was most valuable because it blended philosophy and religion. The poet's faith she judged even "more restful" in his later poems than in his earlier ones,[8] but she felt that the primary value of his philosophic teaching was to show the world that "to make use of the things of time to sustain us as we look upward, this is our wisdom during our life here, ere the disembodied Psyche can soar into more ethereal regions, and revel in the sunlight...."[9]

In the same year Sidney Herbert Mellone published a series of lectures on five leaders of religious thought during the nineteenth century. The essays placed Robert Browning in the company of Auguste Comte, Cardinal Newman, Herbert Spencer, and James Martineau. Moreover, the lectures had been delivered at the Divinity School of Meadville, Pennsylvania. The thesis of the essay on Browning is that the poet's

[6]*Ibid.,* p. 144.
[7]Dorothea Beale, "Christmas Eve," *Literary Studies of Poems, New and Old* (London, 1902), p. 111.
[8]*Ibid.,* p. 102.
[9]*Ibid.,* p. 84.

approach to the problems of life was predicated upon a philosophy of experience rather than one of reason. According to Mellone, reason showed Browning "No road to fresh positive truth in things human or divine" and therefore the poet assumed a position of deep, but not absolute, scepticism concerning reason.[10] But the value of this philosophy Mellone believed to consist in a call to the individual to recognize

> the value of work—that is, effort and energy of spirit—in deepening experience and so affording new data for knowledge. His appeal is to the completest human experience tested and interpreted by Work,—active productive energy of the spirit is the way to the meaning of things.[11]

There is in this statement, of course, an interpretation of Browning's message which relates it, surprisingly enough, to Carlyle and his Doctrine of Work. Mellone saw the usefulness of Browning's philosophy of energy and work in its application to the problem of evil in the world. It would transform evil into good, not by destruction, but by reconstruction.[12] Since Mellone claimed that "what is simply *bad* cannot be worked out," by his interpretation the materials which make up evil would necessarily have to be rearranged to good purpose.[13] Then, too, the writer pointed out the fact that the person who bases his religion on such a philosophy of working things out through personal experience rather than through appeal to authority will find Browning's philosophy valuable, for it will encourage him to work out his religion by expanding the range of his experience.[14]

John A. Hutton, in his *Guidance from Robert Browning in*

[10]Sidney Herbert Mellone, "Robert Browning," *Leaders of Religious Thought in the Nineteenth Century* (Edinburgh, 1902), p. 255.
[11]*Ibid.*, p. 254.
[12]*Ibid.*, p. 288.
[13]*Ibid.*, p. 265.
[14]*Ibid.*, p. 293.

Matters of Faith (1903), judged Browning's philosophy of experience far less important than his doctrine of the impassioned moment. To Hutton, the dramatic presentation of these moments—those found in *Pippa Passes* or described in Caponsacchi's monologue in *The Ring and the Book,* for example—constitutes both a "teaching on Conversion," which states that man can "leap to the breast of God" from any depths, and a message "which ranks him with the prophets."[15]

On the other hand, Hutton did not think that Browning's statements about evil ought to be received into the canon of his teachings. He thought that evil was a personal matter to the poet, who "refuses to speak for others . . . will speak only for himself."[16] Despite this statement, Hutton went on to interpret Browning's ideas on the struggle between the forces of good and evil:

> The best is bound to be. Sometimes he [Browning] tries to think the dread alternative, to realize what it would be if all were error. But his mind sickens before that awful prospect, and the poet rightly takes that sickness, that first approach to madness, as corroboration of his instinctive faith in the triumph of God in the fulness of time.[17]

Then, as if to complicate the matter further, Hutton explained that good will triumph over evil only if a certain condition is met, that is, only "if every soul who knows the good will hate and strive against the evil."[18] In terms of salvation, then, every soul will be saved if those who are good will know evil and struggle against it. Lest this seem to be a case in which ignorance is truly bliss, Hutton made it clear that those who do fight the good fight are given an extra measure of

[15]*Guidance from Robert Browning in Matters of Faith* (Edinburgh and London, 1903), pp. 49–50.
[16]*Ibid.,* p. 103.
[17]*Ibid.,* p. 111.
[18]*Ibid.,* p. 115.

reward in that only to them "does life *feel* real and full of promise . . ."[19]

Leslie Stephen did not allow himself to become involved, as Hutton did, in Browning's ideas on good and evil, but in an article in *The Living Age,* he testified to Browning's "amazingly subtle and active understanding,"[20] although warning readers that the poet had been overpraised for poems like *La Saisiaz,* in which "he repeats the most familiar of all arguments about the immortality of the soul, heaven and hell, and so forth, as if they had never occurred to any one before, instead of being the staple of whole libraries of theology."[21]

Perhaps the most interesting of the comments made in praise of Robert Browning in 1905 is that by Dean William Ralph Inge, who devoted thirty-two pages to "The Mysticism of Robert Browning."[22] In order to avoid, if possible, any objections to his including Browning in a book about English mystics, Inge began with a defense of his inclusion of the poet: "We may rightly call him a mystic, in virtue of his profound belief in a perfect spiritual world, in which all broken fragments are made whole, all riddles solved, all legitimate hopes satisfied."[23]

After commenting upon Browning's belief in "the nonexistence of absolute evil," his view of original sin as "a defect imposed on us by God for our final good," Inge made the point that the great law of the universe for Browning is

[19]*Ibid.,* p. 116.

[20]"Browning's Casuistry," *The Living Age,* CCXXXVI (1903), 257.

[21]*Ibid.,* p. 263.

[22]*Studies of English Mystics* (London, 1906), pp. 207–239.

[23]Rather a loose definition, one would think, for it stretches the term *mystic* to include all Christians who have "a profound belief in a perfect spiritual world," etc. In other words, if we accept this definition must we not accept, alongside those like St. Thérèse, Brother Lawrence, and St. Francis, any sincere believer? It is true that the word is difficult to define, but one would think that something more than simple faith alone is involved in mysticism.

the law of love, but sexual love rather than charity.[24] Inge believed that Browning's exposition of this law of love as a means to the final truth made Browning "the hierophant of these new mysteries,"[25] and that "What makes Browning such an original teacher is that none else has believed so wholeheartedly in the advantages of this particular 'pathway to reality,' or has described so completely the ground which we shall traverse if we follow it."[26]

In 1906 *Chambers's Cyclopaedia of English Literature* attempted to summarize the reason for Browning's widespread influence as a thinker:

> Robert Browning is essentially the poet of poets and thinkers. Perhaps more than any other his mind influences the whole trend of the thought of our generation, but it is largely by *influencing the influencers*. Great as his direct influence undoubtedly is, his indirect and unacknowledged power is wider still, through the whole tone of the teaching of leading minds, themselves permeated by his thought.[27]

Unfortunately, this statement is not elaborated upon, for there is a great deal of truth to the proposition that much of Browning's influence was indirect. So too, it must have been with his reputation: that much of it had been gained indirectly. The "influencers"—the Browning Societies, the literary critics, the teachers, the ministers, and others like them—must have helped greatly in the spreading of his reputation as a thinker.

The lecture given by Frank W. Gunsaulus to the class of 1907 at Chicago Theological Seminary, later published as a chapter in *The Higher Ministries of Recent English Poetry*, is

[24]*Ibid.,* pp. 214–219.
[25]*Ibid.,* p. 221.
[26]*Ibid.,* p. 222.
[27]Jeanie Morison, "Robert Browning and Elizabeth Barrett Browning," *Chambers's Cyclopaedia of English Literature,* ed. David Patrick (London, 1906), III, 558–559.

a good example of the spreading of Browning's reputation by an influencer. To this class of prospective ministers—themselves influencers—Gunsaulus said of the poet, "I look upon him in the midst of the lights and shadows of our rationalism, as the prophet of the age of reason,—not Voltaire's age of reason, but the Christ's."[28] Calling him "Deeper than Arnold"[29] and "the best teacher for us now,"[30] Gunsaulus described Browning as "a philosopher who goes beneath the achievement of science"[31] and

> ... a man who has subtlety of mind sufficient to understand Hegel and Fichte and Schelling with power enough to teach the idealism of Germany as its waves reach again and again unto our shores, a still deeper idealism.[32]

Such praises of Browning's thought from the mouth of an inspiring speaker might well be expected to have had a lasting impression on the hearers and perhaps a wider indirect influence upon their future congregations. It was probably such statements as those by Gunsaulus that prompted W. J. Dawson to write: "... to the first minds of the age, the men who lead and govern the world of thought, Browning has been and is a potent and inspiring force."[33]

One of the more interesting commentaries upon the thought of Robert Browning was published in 1907 in *Cornhill Magazine* by Frederick M. Padelford, who therein reported the results of a class he had taught in Victorian poetry at the University of Washington.[34] Padelford stated that his students

[28]"Robert Browning," *The Higher Ministries of Recent English Poetry* (New York, 1907), p. 191.
[29]*Ibid.*, p. 232.
[30]*Ibid.*, p. 180.
[31]*Ibid.*, p. 204.
[32]*Ibid.*, p. 181.
[33]*The Makers of English Poetry* (New York, 1906), p. 276.
[34]"Browning Out West," *Cornhill Magazine*, N. S. XXII (1907), 253–262.

had become so enthusiastic over Browning that the two weeks he had proposed to devote to Browning were extended to a full semester's course in his poetry. Moreover, his students would have worked on Browning another semester had their professor allowed.[35] What makes the enthusiasm of these college students for Browning even more important to this study is Padelford's suggestion that a primary reason for the popularity of Browning at the University of Washington was his philosophy of life. Padelford wrote about his students:

> Predisposed to action, and optimistic by temperament, they readily and heartily accept a philosophy which says that the spiritual life also is a conflict, and a conflict in which there must be eventual triumph. To many, acquaintance with Browning means the revival of faith through the glad discovery that the spiritual life can be led without compromising the intellectual—indeed can only be adequately lived when co-operating with the intellectual.[36]

Further, Padelford asserted that many people learned from Browning that spiritual life is "the very essence of all living," and that in this recognition they recovered lost faith.[37] These observations led Padelford to rejoice that "What one of our brightest essayists[38] has happily termed 'The Browning Tonic' is permeating society."[39]

If it were true that the tonic was "permeating society," we may be certain that such benevolent influences as those exercised by Padelford were instrumental in spreading the tonic about. His report is probably too modest, for he failed to give himself any credit for Browning's popularity among the stu-

[35]*Ibid.*, pp. 257–258.
[36]*Ibid.*, pp. 261–262.
[37]*Ibid.*, p. 262.
[38]Martha Baker Dunn, "The Browning Tonic," *The Atlantic Monthly,* XC (1902), 208.
[39]Padelford, p. 254.

dents. It is quite probable that his excellent teaching of and enthusiasm for Browning kindled the interest of the students in the poet. Padelford, like Gunsaulus, represents another instance of a definite but unmeasurable influence upon Browning's reputation as a thinker. And yet we may feel sure that his case was not unique nor, perhaps, even rare. There must have been many another teacher or lecturer who passed his love for Browning on to his hearers, but the substance of whose remarks never found a way into print.

Most of the writers who considered Browning's thought between 1900 and 1909 were neither image-worshippers nor iconoclasts. Perhaps the four most important full-length studies of Browning published during this period[40] best illustrate the moderate attitude, one that found both strengths and serious weaknesses in Browning's thought.

Stopford Brooke deplored the fact that "Browning's theology and ethics, as they are called, have been discussed at wearying length for the last ten years. . . ."[41] And further, he refused to side wholly with the most enthusiastic admirers of Browning by admitting not only that Browning really was obscure but, what was even more heretical, that the poet's obscurity arose from his style, not from "any exceptional depth of thought or by any specially profound analysis of the soul . . ."[42]

[40]Stopford A. Brooke, *The Poetry of Robert Browning* (New York, 1902) ; Gilbert Keith Chesterton, *Robert Browning* (London, 1903) ; Edward Dowden, *Robert Browning* (London, 1904) ; and C. H. Herford, *Robert Browning* (Edinburgh, 1905).

[41]Brooke, p. 38.

[42]*Ibid.*, p. 50. In reviewing the books of Brooke and Chesterton, F. Greenslet still saw in the former too much of the Browning fever, despite Brooke's attempt to point out the poet's faults. "New Lights on Browning," *The Atlantic Monthly*, XCII (1903), 420. William Peterfield Trent, on the other hand, praised both authors, commenting that ". . . it begins to look as if Browning criticism were no longer under the control of framers of handbooks and introductions to a mysterious tract of literature, of the compilers of Browning cyclopaedias, and of

G. K. Chesterton called Browning's religious opinions "very sticking and very solid"[43] and traced in some detail the most important of Browning's convictions, the doctrine of the imperfection of man and a hope in an "imperfect" God, that is, a God who, seeing man suffering, is seized by a kind of divine jealousy not to be outdone and becomes man to be crucified so that He can share man's sufferings.[44] Chesterton blithely agreed with critics who held that Browning's optimism was based upon emotions, but, with a characteristic flash of paradox, he called this emotional optimism a virtue rather than a vice.[45] On the other hand, Chesterton rejected for Browning the reputation of "pure intellectualism," which he felt had been mistakenly based on the poet's love of casuistry.[46] If, as Greenslet averred,[47] this study by Chesterton "shows unmistakably the direction of the literary wind," the direction in which Chesterton seemed to be pointing was toward a fuller consideration of Browning the poet than of Browning the thinker.

This point was brought out in 1905 by Edward Dowden, who wrote that Browning's "thought, as far as it is polemical, will probably cease to interest readers."[48] Also, although he could praise the poet's optimism as "a part of the vigorous sanity of his moral nature," Dowden found Browning's *Christmas-Eve* "crude . . . in misconception" of the beliefs of the Roman

---

the elaborate dissertations upon the 'Digressions in Sordello' and other such abstruse topics." "Two Estimates of Browning," *Forum*, XXXV (1903), 297.

[43]Chesterton, p. 177.
[44]*Ibid.*, pp. 178–179.
[45]*Ibid.*, p. 183.
[46]*Ibid.*, p. 193. In 1901, writing for the *Daily News*, Chesterton had called Browning "a thinker, but . . . not primarily a thinker." "Browning and His Ideal," *A Handful of Authors*, ed. Dorothy Collins (New York, 1953), p. 94.
[47]See note 42.
[48]Dowden, p. 397.

Catholic church and censured the poet for failing to consider fairly religious beliefs other than his own.[49]

C. H. Herford discovered that Browning's "imagination was a factor in his apprehension of truth"[50] and that much of his teaching came from sources other than his own mind:

> ... much of it [his teaching] was derived from traditions of which he never shook himself clear; much from the exercise of a speculative reason which, though incomparably agile, was neither well disciplined in its methods nor particularly original in its grasp of principles. But with the vitalising heart of his faith neither tradition nor reasoning had so much to do as that logic of the imagination by which great poets often implicitly enunciate what the after-thinker slowly works out.[51]

But Herford also saw Browning's conflicting views of the after-life[52] and the idealization of effort by which he "transferred the focus of interest and importance from 'the next world's reward and repose' to the vital 'struggles in this.' "[53] In addition he saw Browning's exaltation of love as a means of avoiding the good versus evil dilemma, "the nearest approach to a solution of that conflict which Browning's mechanical metaphysics permitted."[54]

In addition to the favorable and moderate criticisms which made their appearance during this decade, a substantial body of adverse comments found a way into print between 1900 and 1909. By no means as numerous in any part of this decade as the favorable critics, the adverse critics showed their

---

[49]*Ibid.*, p. 129. Inge too had pointed out this fault of treating antagonistic views unfairly. *Studies of English Mystics,* p. 222.

[50]Herford, p. 285.

[51]*Ibid.*, p. 286.

[52]*Ibid.*, p. 292.

[53]*Ibid.*, p. 294.

[54]*Ibid.*, p. 301.

greatest strength during the earlier years. After 1905 the writers who did not admire Browning for his philosophy were comparatively silent. During the first few years, however, Browning was taken severely to task for what the critics thought were his failings as a serious thinker.

The first of the attacks upon Browning during this period was perhaps the most sweeping. In his *Interpretations of Poetry and Religion* (1900), George Santayana included a study of Robert Browning and Walt Whitman under the chapter-heading, "The Poetry of Barbarism."[55] The attack therein made on Browning's philosophy of life has been called by William Clyde DeVane "the most devastating criticism which Browning has encountered."[56] Santayana began by defining his key term, *barbarism*:

> For the barbarian is the man who regards the passions as their own excuse for being; who does not domesticate them either by understanding their cause or by conceiving their ideal goal. He is the man ... who merely feels and acts, valuing in his life its force and its filling, but careless of its purpose and its form. His delight is in abundance and vehemence; his art, like his life, shows an exclusive respect for quantity and splendour of materials. His scorn for what is poorer and weaker than himself is only surpassed by his ignorance of what is higher.[57]

Browning's mind displayed the presence "of a barbaric genius, of a truncated imagination, of a thought and art inchoate and ill-digested, of a volcanic eruption that tosses itself quite blindly and ineffectually into the sky."[58] In rapid succession, Santayana attacked Browning's philosophy, his moral ideal,

[55]*Interpretations of Poetry and Religion* (New York, 1900), pp. 166–216.
[56]*A Browning Handbook*, 2nd ed. (New York, 1955), p. 587.
[57]Santayana, pp. 176–177.
[58]*Ibid.*, p. 189.

and his religious position, especially as this last touches upon immortality. Browning's metaphysics the critic deplored for its lack of order and its failure to achieve results. He judged the poet's moral teaching faulty in that Browning seems to glory in energy without being much concerned with the purposes of the energy. And finally, he censured Browning for concluding that an incomplete life here on earth is a sufficient argument that there will be another in which all things will be made complete.[59]

Santayana was not unaware of qualities in Browning's thought and poetry which could hold an attraction for those who wished to find a formal philosophy in his poetry, and against such attractions Santayana issues the following warning:

> There is a serious danger that a mind gathering from his [Browning's] pages the raw material of truth, the unthreshed harvest of reality, may take him for a philosopher, for a rationalizer of what he describes. Awakening may be mistaken for enlightenment, and the galvanizing of torpid sensations and impulses for wisdom.
> Against such fatuity reason should raise her voice.[60]

As one might expect from the foregoing quotations, Browning's views on love were bound to fall under the disapproving gaze of the Spanish-born philosopher. Santayana argued that love is always a passion to Browning and that his love never rises to the spiritual heights of contemplative love.[61] Another facet of Browning's thought that seemed especially repugnant to Santayana is the poet's preference for emotion, feeling, or intuition to the power of reason. Santayana complained that, although Browning was a gatherer of phenomena and a man

[59]*Ibid.*, pp. 189–190.
[60]*Ibid.*, p. 191.
[61]*Ibid.*, p. 195. Cf. Inge's statement that love in Browning is nearly always *eros*.

of wide experience, he never tried to fit these gatherings into a rational system. Perhaps his chief failure as a thinker, according to Santayana, was the fact that "No conception could be farther from his thought than the essential conception of any rational philosophy, namely, that feeling is to be treated as raw material for thought. . . ."[62] This same complaint was given voice again a few pages later in the statement that Browning "had no thought of subjugating impulses into the harmony of reason. He did not master life, but was mastered by it."[63]

As one might expect, Santayana could not overlook Browning's statements about immortality, which even some of his ardent supporters had found at least ambiguous. Browning's idea of immortality and the future life he found

> . . . in a spirit the direct opposite of the philosophic maxim of regarding the end, of taking care to leave a finished life and a perfect character behind us. It is the opposite, also, of the religious *memento mori*, of the warning that the time is short before we go to our account. According to Browning, there is no account: we have an infinite credit. With an unconscious and characteristic mixture of heathen instinct with Christian doctrine, he thinks of the other world as heaven, but of the life to be led there as the life of nature.[64]

Santayana rejected, then, any view of an eternity which presented eternal life as an infinite extension of earthly activity. Eternal happiness to him consisted of the eternal contemplation of God. Browning, on the other hand, hardly endorsed

---

[62]*Ibid.*, p. 198.

[63]*Ibid.*, p. 200. This failure to "master life" and to discipline self, to subjugate the passions to reason, represents one of the chief weaknesses Santayana finds common to Browning and Whitman. The "barbaric yawp" consists in an unconscious boasting about the failure to subject experience to reason.

[64]*Ibid.*, p. 203.

such ideas, and Santayana saw in the poet's conception of eternity a real weakness in his doctrine of imperfection:

> ...if Browning had had the idea of perfecting and rationalizing this life rather than of continuing it indefinitely, he would have followed Aristotle and the Church[65] in this matter of eternity as contemplation of the Beatific Vision of God. But he had no idea of anything eternal; and so he gave, as he probably would have said, a filling to the empty Christian immortality by making every man busy in it about many things.[66]

Lest it be argued that Browning saw eternity as a perpetual development of man's soul, Santayana objected:

> But it is a mere euphemism to call this perpetual vagrancy a development of the soul, a development means the unfolding of a definite nature, the gradual manifestation of a known idea. A series of phases, like the successive leaps of a waterfall, is no development. And Browning has no idea of an intelligible good which the phases of life might approach and with reference to which they might constitute a progress.[67]

Thus Browning's ideas of eternity either as a perpetuation of the infinite moment of happiness—as expressed in the final verses of *The Last Ride Together*—or as a continuation of life's struggle—as expressed in *Rabbi Ben Ezra* and the *Epilogue* to *Asolando*—are both seen by Santayana as the outgrowths of a mind which could not fit phenomena into a meaningful system, and which failed completely to rise above an animal—a barbaric—concept of immortality.

[65]Santayana was only nominally a Catholic himself, "as a matter of sympathy and traditional allegiance, not of philosophy," he wrote. *The Philosophy of Santayana,* ed. Irwin Edman (New York, 1936), p. 5.

[66]*Interpretations of Poetry and Religion,* p. 204.

[67]*Ibid.*

Although other writers might have taken Browning for a defender of Christianity, Santayana thought Browning's version of Christianity both pernicious and un-Christian because he based his religion more upon experience and temperament than upon revelation and reason:

> And what does temperament say? That life is an adventure, not a discipline; that the exercise of energy is the absolute good, irrespective of motives or of consequences. These are the maxims of a frank barbarism . . . The vague religion which seeks to justify this attitude is really only another outburst of the same irrational impulse.
>
> In Browning this religion takes the name of Christianity, and identifies itself with one or two Christian ideas arbitrarily selected; but at heart it has far more affinity to the worship of Thor or of Odin than to the religion of the Cross. The zest of life becomes a cosmic emotion; we lump the whole together and cry "Hurrah for the Universe." . . . such the passions on which it feeds.[68]

If Browning's thought had fared badly in the hands of Santayana, it fared little better in those of John M. Robertson in 1903. There is more than a touch of acridity in Robertson's statements, a defect which might well alienate many readers and cause them to ignore Robertson's objections, some of which seem well taken. Almost nothing in Browning's philosophy of life seems to have suited the author of *Browning and Tennyson as Teachers: Two Studies*. It is the "vivacious empiricism of an egoist of literary genius,"[69] and the poet is "an inefficient intelligence in a sphere of thought in which he insisted on instructing his fellows."[70] More specifically, Robertson attacked Browning's belief that sin and evil are not real,

[68]*Ibid.*, p. 207.
[69]John M. Robertson, *Browning and Tennyson as Teachers: Two Studies* (London, 1903), p. 155.
[70]*Ibid.*, p. 128.

his statements on immortality, and his approach to serious thought.

The first of these three matters Robertson centered around the Pope's soliloquy in *The Ring and the Book,* especially the statement that God "unmakes but to remake," that is, that Guido will be remade by God:

> That is not the Pope's final philosophy only. It is Robert Browning's. And what a philosophy ... It is only a humanized version of the mythus of hell and purgatory: even more naively than they, it negates the very assumption on which it stands, the infinitude of Deity. This conception of Omnipotence as an artificer who chronically makes a misfit, so to speak, what is it but primeval puerility made to look profound?[71]

Browning's conception of eternity as endless growth, Robertson described as "a quasi-idea of the perpetual expansion of a finite intelligence toward infinity"[72] and called it "as profitable a mental exercise as imagining an infinite succession of ciphers filling up infinite space."[73] Finally, the author implied that at the root of Browning's difficulties as a serious thinker was his unwillingness or inability to take the trouble to understand the philosophic problems which he raised. Such conclusions as the poet came to with his approach to philosophy, the intellect, and knowledge, Robertson stamped as utterly worthless[74] and concluded that "the very acceptance by Christians of Browning's quasi-concrete theology is an admission of the breakdown of their own."[75]

71*Ibid.,* p. 115.
72*Ibid.,* p. 154.
73*Ibid.*
74*Ibid.,* p. 155. "His endless talk about God is as valuable as Victor Hugo's spontaneous intuitions about Scotch geography, English names, and the poetry of Goethe and Schiller."
75*Ibid.,* p. 157.

The adverse criticism of Browning as a thinker was not as strong after 1905 as it was before. The adverse critics were not only less vocal, but perhaps also less effective, than their counterparts during the early years of this decade; and, further, they numbered among them no philosophical critic of Santayana's stature. Only two writers of importance seem to have registered objections to Browning's thought between 1906 and 1909.

The first of these critics, Alfred Benn, emphasized weaknesses in Browning's mental process and philosophical background:

> With most of his admirers Browning passes for a great philosopher; but his intellect had nothing of the logical or scientific strain, nor was his reading, though wide, likely to bring it into contact with the critical results of contemporary thought.[76]

Benn further implied a failure of Browning's intellect when he wrote that the poet's solution of the problems of life and faith as it is presented in *Christmas-Eve and Easter-Day*—a solution which Benn interpreted as advice to enjoy this life and be hopeful about the next—displays an inability on the part of the poet to judge the value of his own conclusions and a confusing conflict between his artistic temperament and his early religious training.[77]

The second critic, Helen A. Clarke, was basically friendly to the poet, but in her *Browning's England* (1908) she supplied another instance of what she considered a failure of Browning's intellectual attitude. She censured the poet for his being unable not only to accept, but even to understand, the arguments of such groups as the Catholics and the Tractar-

[76]Alfred William Benn, *The History of English Rationalism in the Nineteenth Century* (London, 1906), II, 275.
[77]*Ibid.*, pp. 276–277.

ians. Browning always took, she argued, "the ordinary ground of the opposition, that in using such arguments they must be insincere, and they must be perfectly conscious of their insincerity."[78]

Surveying the evidence in this essay, one can readily see that Browning's supporters far outnumbered those who stood against him. On the other hand, it can also be seen that there was a substantial body of adverse opinion formed and forming, and there were clear indications that rougher waters lay ahead for Browning's thought. Another point to be kept in mind is that, despite its severity and its source, the attack of Santayana on Browning seems to have been met by neither loud hurrahs nor catcalls; its effect on the other criticisms of the decade seems hardly perceptible, a matter the more surprising because the philosopher-critic voiced a great number of objections which will be seen again in later decades in the same or slightly different dress. Whatever the reasons, it is clear that Santayana's criticism did little else than ruffle the waters during the early years of this decade and that those who admired Browning's thinking during the years 1900–1909 were in command of the situation at the end of the decade nearly as well as they had been at the close of the nineteenth century.

[78]Helen A. Clarke, *Browning's England* (New York, 1908), p. 347. Benn (p. 280) wrote that Browning showed "bitter hostility . . . without parallel in English poetry" towards the Catholic church. For a detailed study of this matter, see Boyd Litzinger, *Robert Browning and the Babylonian Woman* (*Baylor Browning Interests,* No. 19 [Waco, Texas, 1962]).

Such sought utterance, and had a right to find it—there was an end. ✿ BROWNING'S ESSAY ON CHATTERTON

A CENTENNIAL

THERE HAD BEEN A CERTAIN INSTAbility in Browning's reputation as a thinker in the first decade of this century. The charges made by George Santayana had for a moment shaken the structure of the reputation Browning's supporters had been joyfully raising. The immediate effect, however, was not to destroy the edifice of praise, but to rock it, and by the beginning of the second decade the half-completed monument had steadied enough to allow the workers to begin again adding courses and tiers to Browning's reputation for serious thought.

Not the least of the steadying and favorable influences during the years 1910–1919 was the centenary celebration of Browning's birth. The literature published about Browning in 1912 is voluminous, and, as might be expected, most of it is highly favorable to every aspect of the poet's work. It seems almost as though every teacher of Browning, every minister who admired him, and every member of the Browning coterie felt it his bounden duty to put into print some praise, large or small, of the poet. As a result, this plethora of praise contains a considerable amount of material concerned with Browning's message or philosophy, and, if it does not overwhelm, at least it dwarfs the unfavorable criticism of Browning's thought. The progress the adverse critics had made during the first decade of this century was at least offset, if not undone, by the favorable view of Browning's thought presented during the early years of the second decade.

One critic writing in 1910—Edward M. Chapman—ought

to be mentioned here because he found Browning's philosophy of life both wholesome and appealing to the modern mind. He praised "the vast wealth of his intellectual and spiritual resources"[1] and called "the multitude of Browning Societies" evidence that the poet's philosophy and religion were matters of considerable contemporary interest.[2] Chapman believed that an additional reason for the popularity of Browning's thought was the poet's use of the "philosophical method now particularly known as Humanism or Pragmatism."[3] This pragmatic note is pointed up, he wrote, by the fact that Browning taught that "Religion is as necessary and wholesome to a man's soul as bread to his body."[4]

Other favorable critics whose comments reached print before 1912 include Emily Hickey and Thomas R. Lounsbury, the latter in his book, *The Early Literary Career of Robert Browning*. Because of the limitations of his subject it is only natural that Lounsbury did not go deeply into Browning's philosophy of life or his reputation as a thinker. He did, however, mention Browning's intellectual gifts, in relation to the subject of obscurity in his poetry. Blaming the obscurity in certain of Browning's poems on faulty technical artistry and difficult grammatical constructions, Lounsbury insisted "There is no question as to his profound intellectual power."[5] "His thought," continued the writer, "always worth considering, often profound, frequently failed to get itself clothed in adequate expression. This peculiarity is most noticeable in the pieces in which the intellect is acting as pure intellect and not under the stress of emotion."[6] The implication, then, is that

[1] Edward M. Chapman, *English Literature in Account with Religion* (London, 1910), p. 353.

[2] *Ibid.*, p. 389.

[3] *Ibid.*, p. 392.

[4] *Ibid.*, p. 393.

[5] *The Early Literary Career of Robert Browning* (New York, 1911), p. 174.

[6] *Ibid.*, p. 180.

there is no real fault with Browning's thinking, only that he was not always able to give his thoughts clear expression when he was not involved emotionally with them.

In her article "Glorious Robert Browning" (1911) Emily Hickey made two points of value to this study, one a report of the current intellectual repute of the poet and the other an explanatory defense of the morality seemingly advocated by Browning in *The Statue and the Bust*. Let us look first at the latter. Since the weak-willed lovers in *The Statue and the Bust* are chided for not having fulfilled their desires, more than one person has complained that Browning was encouraging immorality. Miss Hickey's defense is not altogether direct, but it is a shrewd cut, resting as it does on the moral attitude of the father of the Protestant Reformation, whom Browning himself had called "Grand rough old Martin Luther."[7] "Have we not here," she asked, "the spirit of *Pecca Fortiter?* A strong sinning would, it seems here, have been better than a weak abstinence from it."[8] Realizing, however, that not all readers would be satisfied by such a defense of Browning's morality, Miss Hickey adds that Browning does not always preach *pecca fortiter,* but that "as a rule Browning lays stress not on the breaking of any part of the law for the sake of fulfilling another part, but on rising to the truest obedience to law through impulse and passion; through the nobility of that impulse and the glory of that passion."[9]

But even more important to this study than her explanation of Browning's moral teaching is her quotation from an unidentified source:

Browning is coming every day more and more into his own. One can scarcely hear a sermon or a speech from a really

[7]*The Complete Poetical Works of Robert Browning,* ed. Horace E. Scudder (Boston, 1895), p. 266. The quotation is from the poem *The Twins.*

[8]Emily Hickey, "Glorious Robert Browning," *The Nineteenth Century and After,* LXX (1911), p. 760.

[9]*Ibid.,* p. 761.

thoughtful preacher or speaker that does not show his influence, either in direct quotation, or in the saying of what is plainly due to that influence.[10]

If Browning's influence had been as strong on nearly every "really thoughtful preacher or speaker" as the above quotation claims, then very healthy indeed must have been the poet's reputation for dealing with weighty matters of philosophical import. And to examine the materials pertinent to this subject published in 1912 is to be convinced that the "man who knows" knew.

A number of the favorable critics in 1912 gave Browning's philosophical or religious message the heady praise of claiming that it either had been or could be a great aid to those in need of spiritual or intellectual succor, although not all of the commentators read his message alike or emphasized the same matters in that message. For example, in his *Some Influences in Modern Philosophic Thought,* Arthur Twining Hadley described life as a struggle between the forces of vitality and those of repression. The man of action, wrote Hadley, will cling to Browning, for his "is poetry which will help him understand his place in that struggle and inspire him to accept its burdens."[11] Darrell Figgis, on the other hand, saw Browning's greatness in the aid he can give to his followers along other lines:

> ... if to help us to stand equipped in manliness and womanliness, loving Beauty and seeing Truth, ripe in sympathy and understanding, be any measure of greatness, then, even apart from all else, we must echo Landor and say, "Browning, a great poet, a very great poet indeed."[12]

Philip S. Moxom, like Emily Hickey, linked Browning with

[10]*Ibid.,* p. 753.
[11]*Some Influences in Modern Philosophic Thought* (New Haven, 1912), p. 96.
[12]Darrell Figgis, *Studies and Appreciations* (London, 1912), p. 88.

Luther and pointed out the fact that Browning gave necessary sustenance to his generation, the corollary being that an acceptance of his ebullient optimism would also be good for the generation struggling in 1912. "This persistent optimism," declared Moxom,

> nourished by deep reflection as well as by faith, makes Browning the "Greatheart" whose words, like Luther's, are "half-battles" emancipating many a soul from doubt and fear and sending a strong pulse of life into a generation which had grown spiritually anaemic under the influence of a prevailing materialism.[13]

Perhaps more personal is the praise given Browning's thought by J. Churton Collins, who saw Browning as a teacher of fundamental Christianity: "But for how many of us has Browning sent new life-blood pulsing into the old truths; for how many of us has he rekindled lights that were becoming dim and taught us to understand and feel what Christianity *really means!*"[14] The attitudes of Collins and Moxom are very closely related, for the tribute of the one to a Browning who rekindled the candles of faith and the accolade of the other to a Browning who overcame spiritual anemia are very nearly identical.

But even more enthusiastic are the words of praise written by A. Austin Foster in his *The Message of Robert Browning* and Helen A. Clarke in her *Browning and His Century*. These two books are especially interesting to this study for the reason that although both authors looked upon Browning as a prophet, they had in mind different sorts of prophets. The poet-prophet presented by Foster is a lineal descendent of his counterparts in the Old Testament. Miss Clarke's, however,

[13]Philip Stafford Moxom, *Two Masters: Browning and Turgenief* (Boston, 1912), p. 42.

[14]*The Posthumous Essays of John Churton Collins*, ed. L. C. Collins (London, 1912), p. 228.

is a prophet of modern philosophy, Spencerian philosophy in particular. Also, as the titles of the two books presage, *The Message of Robert Browning* has about it the tone of religious enthusiasm, whereas *Browning and His Century* displays more of an attempt at a scholarly, scientific approach, reflecting Miss Clarke's desire to show how the poet represented the very best and most advanced thought of the *avant-garde*. For the moment, however, we must consider the recommendations these two authors made to the public concerning the real aid an acceptance of Browning's philosophy can bring.

For Foster, an understanding of Browning's message in two poems—*The Boy and the Angel* and *The Statue and the Bust* —can be a great aid to those in need of spiritual guidance. *The Boy and the Angel,* with its story of the youngster whose simple song was more pleasing to God than either his later service as pope or the song of the angel who tried to fill the young singer's shoes, drew forth this exhortation from the author of *The Message of Robert Browning:*

> Courage then, my brothers! The world needs you: God needs you. Your lives, seemingly so small, are of infinite value; ... It takes a man to do a man's work and an angel to do an angel's. Man, man's way; the angel, the angel's way; each in his own way—and God is satisfied.[15]

The Statue and the Bust is recommended for its tonic value, but the recommendation has about it a note of caution. The theme of the poet, wrote Foster, "is the truth that half-heartedness is unworthy of humanity. Poor, limping hesitating lives are the weak links in the chain of existence, unsatisfying to man, unpardonable by God."[16] But the great message of help to be derived from a reading of the poem, Foster proclaimed in these words:

[15]A. Austin Foster, *The Message of Robert Browning* (New York, 1912), p. 54.
[16]*Ibid.,* p. 143.

When the Eternal Moments of Life come to us, when strong decisions have to be made that cast the issues for the future days, let us make them whole-heartedly and perform them valiantly, being resolved what to do, and having the moral courage to do it—only let it be for the defeat of crime and the exaltation of Righteousness.[17]

The admonition at the end of the quoted passage probably indicates that although Foster found value in "strong decisions," he would rather have led those decisions in directions different from the one suggested in *The Statue and the Bust*.

Helen A. Clarke was not so much interested in Browning the soul-stirrer as she was in Browning the leader and stimulator of modern thought. Of his intellectual approach to religion and the religious controversy raging in his own day, she wrote that he, "far more than Tennyson, put religious speculation upon a basis where it may stand irrespective of a belief in the revelations of historical Christianity."[18] Further she called Browning "the poet who has given the world the utmost certainty of God, the soul and immortality, and the most inspiring ideals of human love."[19] Thus, for Miss Clarke, Browning was the savior of Christianity, albeit a Christianity stripped of "supernaturalism." Of her analysis of Browning as a creative theological thinker more will be said later.

The praise that often accrued by association to Browning's thought was not absent in 1912. Indeed, the critics compared Browning favorably with poets, theologians, and philosophers alike. The bringing together of the names of Browning and Martin Luther by Emily Hickey and Philip S. Moxom has already been shown, and brief reference has been made to Helen A. Clarke's seeing a relationship between Herbert

[17]*Ibid.*, pp. 150–151.
[18]Helen A. Clarke, *Browning and His Century* (New York, 1912), p. 359.
[19]*Ibid.*, p. 370.

Spencer and the poet. A word or two more, however, about this similarity might be in order here. The points of likeness Miss Clarke writes about are several and include attitudes toward knowledge, the evolution of the soul, and evolutionary concepts in general. Of the first, the author of *Browning and His Century* found Spencer and Browning in agreement "that ultimate knowledge is beyond the grasp of the intellect."[20] On the second point a fuller note of praise is sounded in that "Browning seems intuitively to have perceived the fundamental truths of social and psychic evolution at the early age of twenty-five—truths which the philosopher [Spencer] worked out only after years of laborious study."[21] The matter of Browning's intuitive faculty is again brought up in reference to the third matter, Browning's quick appreciation of general evolution, a conception which "was later to be elaborated fully on its objective or observational side by Spencer—the philosopher par excellence of evolution."[22] But Miss Clarke finds other names of prominence in the world of thought with which to connect Browning's in a way which reflects credit upon the poet, writing that he achieved a synthesis of the intuitional with the scientific, a synthesis "receiving the fullest recognition by such masters of nineteenth-century thought as Theodore Merz and Emile Boutroux."[23]

Two poets and a theologian round out the roll of prominent names with which Browning's thought was associated in 1912. Ernest Hartley Coleridge, in an essay for *The Robert Browning Centenary Celebration* wrote that "Between Browning and Wordsworth there is this in common, that they both were teachers; that both believed that they had a message to

[20]*Ibid.*, p. 26.

[21]*Ibid.*, p. 27.

[22]*Ibid.*, p. 40.

[23]*Ibid.*, pp. 354–355. Joseph Theodore Merz (1840–1922), author of *A History of European Thought in the Nineteenth Century* and *A Fragment on the Human Mind;* Étienne Émile Boutroux (1845–1921), French philosopher and prolific author of books on philosophy.

deliver or a gospel to preach; that both created in order to reveal."[24] Wordsworth is again Browning's companion in Philip S. Moxom's book, but here the older poet fares less well by the comparison. "No other poet," writes Moxom, "not even Wordsworth, has produced so large a body of weighty thought. . . . Everywhere there is an appeal to the intellect; everywhere there is stimulus to thought."[25] It is Moxom also who brought in Calvin in order to show the happy superiority of Browning's optimism over Calvin's gloomy doctrine. In Browning's philosophy, writes Moxom, there is to be found "a divine predestination as fundamental as in that of Calvin, but it is predestination not to perdition but to salvation,—to the fulfillment of life."[26] William Blake, like Calvin, comes off only second best in the eyes of Arthur Twining Hadley:

> Browning has gone back to Blake's conception of vitality as a thing essentially right and essentially necessary; but he avoids Blake's error of linking the name of God with the spirit of repression, and making him the God of only half the world, instead of the whole.[27]

It is not unexpected that the favorable critics in 1912 should have dwelt long on the value of Browning's religious thought and teaching. Again two schools of thought—not wholly reconcilable, but therefore the more interesting—are represented. Whereas A. Austin Foster seems to represent the religious position which relies upon enthusiastic acceptance of so-called "Bible religion," John Churton Collins and Helen A. Clarke represented an opposite extreme—a Christianity akin to that of Matthew Arnold's *St. Paul and Protestantism* and

[24]"Browning and Wordsworth on 'Intimations of Immortality,' " *The Robert Browning Centenary Celebration,* ed. William C. Knight (London, 1912), p. 31.
[25]Moxom, p. 20.
[26]*Ibid.,* p. 36.
[27]Hadley, p. 92.

Literature and Dogma. An espousal of Browning's religious thought by members of both parties is paradoxical, and yet the paradox helps no little to explain Browning's widespread popularity as a thinker during the late nineteenth and early twentieth centuries.

From the very beginning of *The Message of Robert Browning,* Foster's approach to Browning and his religion is quite clear. Like the Biblical prophets, wrote Foster,

> Browning had just as emphatically a message to deliver to the men and women of his age, and for that matter ... to all succeeding ages—a message of Life, of Hope, of Spiritual Realities; ... a message that shall irradiate life, give courage to the faint-hearted, and sustain with a vision of glorious hope all storm-tossed, tried, and tempted souls.[28]

Browning's own philosophy he later described as one of ROBUST MANLINESS and BUOYANT FAITH[29] [the capitals are Foster's], and his religion "the religion of honour and chivalrous courtesy, the religion of tolerance and wide-hearted sympathy, the religion of work and self-sacrifice, the religion of hope and inspiration, the religion of God's own gentlemen."[30]

Collins' attitude toward Browning's religious thought makes him a link between the positions of Foster and Miss Clarke. Collins argued that Browning would have been willing to admit that historically Christianity was more myth than fact, but that the admission would not have made Browning less a Christian, partly because his religious beliefs were matters more soundly based in intuition than on intellect[31] and partly because the poet had adopted "Lessing's theory of a progres-

[28]Foster, p. 5.
[29]*Ibid.,* pp. 9, 13.
[30]*Ibid.,* p. 177.
[31]Collins, *Posthumous Essays,* pp. 228 ff.

sive revelation," one that may have been faulty and incomplete in its beginnings.[32]

Collins' approach is like Miss Clarke's in that she saw Browning not as an opponent, but actually an accepter, of the Higher Criticism. According to her, Browning "was familiar with the whole trend of biblical criticism in the first half of the century and its effect upon certain of the orthodox churchmen."[33] But more important is her insistence that Browning is really a friend of the nineteenth-century critics who disputed the accuracy of the Bible. Using *Saul* as an example, she wrote that "In thus making David prophesy of an ideal which had not been evolved at his time, Browning indulges in what the biblical critics would call prophecy after the fact, and so throws himself in on the side of the mythical interpreters of the Bible."[34] Of the same poem, Miss Clarke held that in conceiving in *Saul* "the idea of internal instead of external revelation . . . it will be seen that Browning was in the van of the thought of the century, and still more was he in the van in the psychological tinge which he gives to David's experience."[35] Lest dissenters point to *A Death in the Desert* as proof that Browning was the enemy of the Strausses and Renans of his time, Miss Clarke brought this poem as well into her evidence, saying that it proves Browning's knowledge of the German criticism but that it is nothing more than a dramatic poem, exhibiting St. John's, not Browning's, beliefs.[36] To Miss Clarke, Browning has achieved a synthesis of scientific criticism and intuitive belief. In her words,

> . . . his worth for his age was in saving religion, *not* upon a basis of faith, but upon the ground of logical arguments deduced from the failure of knowledge, of his personal intuition

[32]*Ibid.,* p. 241.
[33]Clarke, p. 51.
[34]*Ibid.,* p. 54.
[35]*Ibid.,* p. 51.
[36]*Ibid.,* pp. 66–71.

of God and his mystical vision in regard to the nature of God. So complete a synthesis is this that only in the present century is its full purport likely to be realized.[37]

That this placing of Browning on the side of Strauss and Renan is quite a change from the usual is evident to anyone who has read even a few of the many explications of Browning's poems dealing with religion. Very few of the interpreters would be willing to agree with Miss Clarke that *Saul* and *A Death in the Desert* prove that Browning accepted the conclusions of the Higher Critics. Miss Clarke overlooked Browning's belief in the divinity of Christ, unorthodox though his rejection of the Redemption motive may have been, and the testimony of the third part of *Christmas-Eve,* in which the German critics are rejected. The fact remains, however, that the author of *Browning and His Century,* in order to prove Browning ahead of his times, found his poetry capable of bearing her interpretation. In this way, Browning became in 1912 many things to many people, and, although he would probably have been surprised to know it, he was made to represent two of the three religious positions he had attempted to describe in *Christmas-Eve :* Foster found him a friend of the worshipers in the Independent Chapel, and Miss Clarke saw him sitting in as an assistant to the Göttingen professor.

The praising comments passed upon individual items in Browning's thought or touching upon miscellaneous aspects of his mind are legion and defy efforts to organize them so that they can be presented neatly and fully. But the picture of Browning's stature as a thinker as his admirers in 1912 conceived it would be both incomplete and inadequate were an attempt not made to indicate the scope and the inclusiveness of the myriad compliments which were heaped upon the poet, ranging from application of the customary adjectives *deep* and *subtle* to comparison with Jesus Christ and His

[37]*Ibid.,* pp. 359–360.

teachings. A sampling of these favorable comments is quite necessary to a full understanding of the appreciation certain vocal critics of 1912 held for Robert Browning's philosophy and message.

Thomas R. Slicer, in his "Browning's Personal Interests," made an issue of the consistency of Browning's "underlying philosophy, which was uttered in 'Pauline,' and uttered not differently in the 'Epilogue,' [to *Asolando*] which his last hour of life produced. His last hours expressed exactly what 'Pauline' outlined. It was a consistent soul."[38] Slicer remarked upon another characteristic of Browning's mind, an unconcern with absolute lucidity of expression. "Now Browning's prime consideration," he wrote, "is to get his thought out. He marks the fact that he belongs to a higher type of teachers in that he is not so much concerned as to how his thought shall appear as that it shall get out. He is indifferent as to the mode of its transmission."[39] Three decades later this same matter of opaque expression would be used by Stewart Walker Holmes to show a fault in Browning's mind,[40] but in 1912 it served only to prove that Browning "belongs to a higher type of teachers." Magnanimity and boldness became attributes of Browning's mind when A. Austin Foster treated *Rabbi Ben Ezra* almost as though it were a pro-Semitic tract. In Foster's words:

> And it is to the poet's eternal credit that in placing the utterance of his maturest wisdom in the mouth of Rabbi Ben Ezra, he has dared to reinstate the race of Jewish people once more in the ranks of the respectable, and to claim for them the atmosphere of a more tolerant charity.[41]

[38]"Browning's Personal Interests," *Addresses Commemorating the Birth of Robert Browning, Delivered Before the New York Browning Society* (New York, 1912 ; hereafter cited as *NYBS Addresses*), p. 29.
[39]*Ibid.*, pp. 23–24.
[40]See pp. 127–128 for Holmes's view.
[41]Foster, p. 24.

The intellectual daring of the poet's mind caught the eye of Ernest Hartley Coleridge, who called Browning "a subtle reasoner," who "neither ignored nor shrank from trains of thought which led away from light and peace."[42] And, of course, the whole force of Helen A. Clarke's *Browning and His Century* is directed at proving that Browning was far in advance of most of the better minds of the nineteenth century.

Other individual teachings, attitudes, or qualities of thought and mind which won welcome for Browning in 1912 include his optimism, his views on immortality, his attitude toward love and the passions, evolution, knowledge, and the soul. J. Herman Randall found optimism the key to Browning's influence on his followers, an optimism which has helped to make him "Great as a Poet, great as a Philosopher, greater still as a man, . . . greatest of all as the vital and permanent influence in our moral and spiritual lives."[43] Further, wrote Randall, through his hopeful philosophy,

> He has rekindled Faith, he has made Love more real and beautiful, he has replenished the fires of Hope and Enthusiasm. He has put iron into the blood and steel into the backbone, and if he has not driven every cloud out of the sky, he has, at least, enabled the modern man to believe that, in spite of every cloud, the sun still shines, and has thus nerved him with new courage to face the solution to every darkest problem.[44]

"The best cure for an attack of pessimism," prescribed Randall, "is a good dose of Browning's buoyant, virile faith and courage."[45] This same optimism was defended by C. T. Winchester. "Nobody," he claimed, "knew better, nobody has painted with more terrible fidelity, the darker phases of

[42]Coleridge, p. 35.
[43]"Browning, the Influence," *NYBS Addresses,* p. 114.
[44]*Ibid.,* pp. 113–114.
[45]*Ibid.,* p. 114.

human life."[46] Browning's belief in immortality was praised by Kate Upson Clark in a context which demands recording here:

> Never since the Man of Galilee has such a spiritual power swayed our earth as dwelt in Robert Browning. Mother, wife and his own soul forced him into the bright battalions. Through the spirit alone, he asserts a thousand times, comes all conquest, all loss. . . . As for faith in immortality, a faith which has done more to ennoble and give divinity to human life than any other one influence, the New Testament itself is not stronger in proclaiming it than Robert Browning.[47]

This extreme opinion makes Winchester's assessment of Browning's exaltation of the power of passion and love appear sheer conservatism. He made a comparatively modest claim that "Nowhere else in English poetry, since Shakespeare let fall the pen with which he had written the last of his tragedies do I find such superb examples of the power of a great passion to energize and uplift the soul as are recorded in the pages of Robert Browning."[48] Dimmed also by Mrs. Clark's astounding praise was Miss Julia Leavens' presidential welcome to the New York Browning Society, with its praise of Browning's "prescience," displayed by the fact that "when but twenty-five years old, he gave to the world the idea of evolution, thirty years before Darwin published his epoch-making book."[49]

The flood of 1912 did not exhaust the store of favorable criticisms in the second decade of this century, but it did deplete the supply somewhat, and praise trailed off rather sharply as the end of the decade approached. From 1912

[46]C. T. Winchester, "Robert Browning," *NYBS Addresses*, p. 76.
[47]Kate Upson Clark, "Browning as a Masquer," *NYBS Addresses*, pp. 93–94.
[48]Winchester, p. 72.
[49]"President's Welcome," *NYBS Addresses*, p. 6.

through 1917, however, the favorable criticism still showed considerable strength, and some writers were nearly as enthusiastic about Browning's thought as the centenary eulogists had been.

In fact, Carolyn F. E. Spurgeon's treatment of Browning in her *Mysticism in English Literature* (1913) fits very nicely into the pattern established in 1912. In her book she compares Browning favorably with such figures as William Blake, William Wordsworth, St. Paul, Plato, and Meister Eckhart. The first two, with Browning, make up "The three great English poets who were also fundamentally mystical in thought."[50] But to Miss Spurgeon, Browning is both philosophical and mystical. "No poet," she wrote

> has a more distinct philosophy of life than Browning. Indeed
> he has as much right to a place among the philosophers, as
> Plato has to one among the poets. Browning is a seer, and
> pre-eminently a mystic; and it is essentially interesting, as in
> the case of Plato and St. Paul, to encounter this latter quality
> as a dominating characteristic of the mind of so keen and
> logical a dialectician. We see at once that the main position of
> Browning's belief is identical with what we have found to be
> the characteristic of mysticism—unity under diversity at the
> centre of all existence.... God is seen in the star, in the
> stone, in the flesh, in the soul and the clod.[51]

Under the general topic of mysticism, Miss Spurgeon mentioned Browning's doctrine of love, his radical rejection of the intellect, and his belief in the illusoriness of evil. Love, she found, is the very key to his mysticism, "the key-note of his work and philosophy" because "he holds it to be the meeting-point between God and man."[52] His views of the conflicts of

[50]Carolyn F. E. Spurgeon, *Mysticism in English Literature* (Cambridge, 1913), p. 34.

[51]*Ibid.,* p. 38.

[52]*Ibid.,* p. 41.

good and evil, intellect and intuition she resolved as logical results of his mysticism. Using *A Pillar at Sebzevah* to illustrate Browning's scepticism, she described him as "at one with Eckhart, and with all mystics, in his appeal from the intellect to that which is beyond the intellect; in his assertion of the supremacy of feeling, intuition, over knowledge."[53] Similarly, she exonerated Browning from fault in his conclusion that evil does not exist but must appear to exist.[54] And thus Carolyn Spurgeon defended three points at which Browning has been attacked—his extreme emphasis on love, his dismissal of the intellect, his paradoxical and contradictory doctrine of evil—by making these characteristics of his alleged mysticism and professing that these are not illogical within the framework of mysticism.

Miss Spurgeon's treatment of Browning on the subject of evil found another expression in the writings of William Lyon Phelps in 1915 and in those of Edward A. G. Hermann a year later. Phelps stressed the impermanent nature of evil in Browning's poetry and philosophy when he explained the closing lines of *Apparent Failure,* saying that "Somewhere, after many ages in the next life, these men will develop into something better under the sunshine of the smile of God."[55] Hermann's explanation of this doctrine, and consequently of Browning's beliefs about the place where sin will be dealt with, is little different. Browning's belief is that hell is not a place of punishment, but "a *spiritual experience,*—the slow or sudden awakening of the sinful soul to a realizing sense of the sinfulness of its sin. Punishment is remedial, not retributive, and it must fulfill its divine purpose here or hereafter."[56]

[53]*Ibid.,* p. 42.
[54]*Ibid.,* p. 44.
[55]*Robert Browning: How to Know Him* (Indianapolis, 1915), p. 361.
[56]Edward A. G. Hermann, *The Faith of Robert Browning* (Boston, 1916), p. 41.

Lilian Whiting, commenting in 1917, held that Browning would "almost place a positive sin above a negative virtue. To live intensely," she continued, "even if sinfully, was to Browning's vision to be on the upward way, rather than to be in a state of negative good."[57] Overlooking, for the moment, the concept of "negative good," we can see that Miss Whiting interpreted Browning's view of evil much as Miss Spurgeon, Phelps, and Hermann did.

Browning's optimism, of course, continued to win favorable comment during the years after 1912. Hermann, in his *The Faith of Robert Browning,* applauded an optimism based not so much upon a reasoned philosophy as upon a religious trust in God. In fact, Hermann seemed to distrust philosophy even more than he thought Browning did, for after writing that Browning "always felt secure because Hope was his anchor, and he came into port grandly because God had been the Captain of his soul,"[58] he went on to deplore Browning's later excursions into abstruse thought:

> It was, no doubt, the consciousness of great intellectual strength that led him, after the death of Mrs. Browning, to wander into the dangerous field of metaphysics, but this latter part of his literary career has been considered as the period of decadence. Much of his last work lacks the intellectual force and moral vigor of his earlier years, and there are weak places where the speculations of the would-be philosopher break down. The cause of this decline has been attributed to failing health and the grief which the poet felt over the loss of his devoted wife, who during her life-time had been the inspiration of his best work.[59]

Despite this breakdown which caused him "to wander into the dangerous field of metaphysics," wrote Hermann, the

[57]*The Brownings: Their Life and Art* (Boston, 1917), p. 124.
[58]Hermann, p. 1.
[59]*Ibid.,* pp. 12–13.

poet "came into the port grandly" because he was "a man of faith" and "one of the greatest exponents of the art of optimism that the world has ever seen."[60] According to Hermann, everyone is coming to an acceptance of Browning's religious optimism:

> If a generation ago unappreciative critics scoffed at the sound of this new voice that was making itself heard in literature, today they place upon the brow of this poet a crown of love. Prominent theologians from the ranks of orthodoxy now find beneath the uneven and unconventional forms of his verse a faith throbbing with the life of God.[61]

The moderate critics, whose comments ranged from mild praise to mild censure, or who merely "explained" Browning's thought, had their say in the period 1910–1919, but the bulk of their writings is quite modest. Especially in and around 1912 was there little room for lukewarmness, for the occasion of the hundredth anniversary of the birth of the poet seems to have challenged the writers to take sides, and those who did not formed a small *tertium quid*. As a result, perhaps, those critics who took neither side strongly sometimes concentrated on explaining, rather than defending or attacking, Browning's individual teachings. J. W. Cunliffe's article on "Browning's Idealism" (1913) might be cited as an example of this method; he explained Browning's idealism, he did not attempt to evaluate it. Cunliffe interpreted various poems to demonstrate Browning's views on the existence of hell, the reality of evil, the divinity of Christ, and the freedom of the will, but only on the matter of the future life did he pass judgment of a very mild sort. He wrote that "As to the nature and extent of the future life, Browning gives only scattered hints of his views, and then it may be doubted whether his characteristic agnosticism would allow us to regard what he

[60] *Ibid.*, p. 14.
[61] *Ibid.*

has said as more than speculation."[62] On other matters, criticism is not in evidence. We are told only that *The Inn Album,* *A Camel Driver,* and *Apparent Failure* show that Browning did not accept a concept of hell as Christian orthodoxy had accepted it. Evil, Browning tells us in *Karshish,* is a mere illusion. Browning's belief in the absolute freedom of man's will is said to be a basic assumption in the poet's whole view of life.[63] Cunliffe used this same approach in another essay, one *PMLA* published in 1912. The sole judgment of Browning's thought is that both Browning and Tennyson compromised their thought to fit their times and that their philosophies seemed outmoded "to the advanced thinkers of our own time," thinkers who are not named.[64] Otherwise, we discover only that Browning was, on the whole, one who had "accepted . . . the orthodox religious position of his time."[65]

George Herbert Clarke's centenary article and Robert H. Fletcher's *Tennyson and Browning: A Manual for College Classes and Other Students* (1913) are, in the main, explanatory. Clarke called Browning a transcendentalist, comparing him with Emerson, but distinguishing him from the American author by saying that "he saw nothing incongruous in the effort to relate the philosophy of idealism to the New Testament narratives as such."[66] *The Statue and the Bust,* we are assured, "makes at root for the righteousness of the race."[67] Despite this eccentricity, Fletcher was neither an enthusiast nor an image-breaker. Like Cunliffe, he dwelt upon Browning's essential idealism, explaining as the reason why Browning

[62]J. W. Cunliffe, "Browning's Idealism," *Transactions of the Wisconsin Academy of Sciences, Arts, and Letters,* XVII (1913), 675.

[63]*Ibid.,* pp. 676–679.

[64]J. W. Cunliffe, "Modern Thought in Meredith's Poems," *PMLA,* XXVII (1912), 14.

[65]*Ibid.,* p. 24.

[66]"Browning and Tennyson: A Browning Centenary Study," *The Canadian Magazine,* XXXIX (1912), 125.

[67]*Ibid.*

chose to examine so many dark and almost morbid subjects that the poet "has made up his mind that idealism and
optimism are of no value unless they can maintain themselves
in the face of all the facts of life."[68]

Now the value of these interpretative critics is not to be
overlooked. Although they did not take sides in the controversy
over Browning the thinker, they did offer guides for readers
who might otherwise have had more than a little difficulty
finding out for themselves what Browning was saying in any
individual poem. On the other hand, insofar as these interpretations were used by readers in place of a careful reading
of Browning's poems, they were harmful, for to that extent
did they prevent the reading public from passing its own
uninfluenced judgment on the poet's thought.

As an aid to understanding Browning, if not to understanding his thought, one work which I have classified as middle-
of-the-road—*The Life of Robert Browning* (1910) by W. Hall
Griffin and Harry Christopher Minchin—was probably of
far greater use than the interpretations and expositions. In
this biography there is no attempt to force upon the readers
an interpretation of poems, nor did the authors consciously
enhance or do violence to Browning's reputation as a philosopher. The very nature of the biography precluded any overt
injection of the writers into the battle about Browning's
thought, for the biographers concentrated more upon the man
than on his poems, more upon his deeds than on his thought.
Beyond this lies a second reason why *The Life of Robert
Browning* does not add significantly to the study at hand:
many of the poems for which Browning's philosophy has been
praised or blamed were written during the years that Griffin did not live to cover, and perhaps the original plan of
the biography would have included more about Browning's
philosophy—or at least more about his reputation for it—
than there appears in the book as we have it.

[68]*Ibid.,* p. 171.

Although the biography does not tell us a great deal about the poet's thought, it does include certain almost casual comments which are of interest here; but even those are marked by moderation and the avoidance of broad judgments. For example, the biographers noted without comment that the poet was an "ardent and consistent theist,"[69] that he considered intuition "superior to proof" in his acceptance of belief in immortality, and that he scorned any idea of eternal punishment.[70] Griffin and Minchin found him "certainly familiar with philosophic theory," but added at once that he probably lacked the patience necessary to the systematic study of philosophy.[71] Perhaps this lack of patience was either a cause or a result of his characteristic thinking, for in that cerebral celerity the biographers discovered the source of the obscurity for which the poet was so often brought to task. They added, finally—and somewhat sadly, one would gather —that Browning "fell, in later days, into metaphysical quagmires, whither already, it is probable, few care to follow him."[72]

Nevertheless, if one were forced to say whether the Griffin and Minchin biography helped or hindered the progress of Browning's reputation as a thinker, he would have to admit that it did no harm and probably even enhanced it somewhat, for the biographers were careful to give numerous examples of the poet's precocity and referred often enough to his wide though unorganized reading in his father's large library. There is nothing in his biography to indicate that the poet was anything less than a cultured, intelligent man; certainly there are none of the disillusioning psychological inferences drawn by Betty Miller.

Other moderate writers during this period serve a transi-

[69]Griffin and Minchin, p. 294.

[70]*Ibid.*, pp. 295, 298. Damnation, the authors found, is attacked in *The Inn Album, Ixion,* and *A Camel Driver.*

[71]*Ibid.*, p. 288.

[72]*Ibid.*, p. 303.

tional function, since most of them leaned away from Browning the thinker. Further, these criticisms set a very curious pattern which we shall observe shortly, in that all of these criticisms were published during the very early years of this decade, most of them before 1912. If we begin by examining the unsigned article in *The Academy* (January 8, 1910), we shall see how these critics felt about Browning's thought. This author phrased his criticism thus:

> His philosophy often seems to be defective. He disparages too much the intellectual faculty, confuses miscellaneous energy with moral strength, and apparently teaches that human love rises by inevitable development into the higher love of God ... [Browning ignores] ... some of the higher aspects and fundamental conditions of the spirit's deeper life, [but] it is a more grateful task to receive with appreciative reverence the large legacy of help and hope that he has left us. If his philosophy be defective, we must remember that the baffling contradictions of experience have never been reduced into clear and consistent harmony by any system of thought that has yet been formed.[73]

The impression is left in the last sentence that the author of this statement did not cast aside Browning's philosophy as worthless, for evidently he felt that its defects are shared by the systems of all other thinkers as well.

The same attitude of qualified praise and blame appears also in Hugh Walker's *The Literature of the Victorian Era* (1910). On the one hand Walker called *Rabbi Ben Ezra* "the embodiment of all that is deepest in Browning's philosophy of religion, and all that is highest in his morality."[74] On the other hand, he judged that in poems like *La Saisiaz* ("neither a great poem nor a philosophic treatise") "The fetters of

[73]"The Poetry of Robert Browning," *The Academy*, LXXVIII (1910), 39.
[74]*Ibid.*, p. 421.

verse cramp the philosophic thought, and the weight of the thought overloads the verse."[75] Walker's greatest objection to Browning's thought, however, was one which touches upon the way the poet's mind seems to have worked:

> Worst of all, perhaps, is his inability to select the essentials and to reject the unimportant. He pours out the whole farrago of his thoughts, and sometimes does not take the trouble to set them in order. . . . he is verbose in the sense that he gives expression to many thoughts when a few would suffice.[76]

The adverse criticisms were almost all voiced during the first three years of this decade, but during these years they were fairly numerous. Had the unfavorable critics maintained after 1912 the frequency with which they had attacked Browning before that time, the picture this decade presents would be radically different from what it is. However, the adverse critics faded even more badly during the last years of the decade than did the favorable ones. Among these critics who did make their voices heard in opposition to Browning's thought were Emily Hickey, Gamaliel Bradford, Henry Jones, and Leslie Stephen.

In 1910 Miss Hickey registered against Browning the complaint that he failed to comprehend things with which he disagreed. In particular she cited his treatment of the Catholic church. She felt that not only could the poet not "feel sympathy with what he called 'imaginative religions':[77] he could not even do them anything like justice."[78] In *The Ring*

[75]*Ibid.,* p. 438.

[76]*Ibid.,* p. 442.

[77]Browning wrote to Elizabeth Barrett: ". . . I don't think I shall let *you* hear, after all, the savage things about Popes and imaginative religions that I must say." *The Letters of Robert Browning and Elizabeth Barrett, 1845–1846* (New York, 1899), I, 6.

[78]Emily Hickey, "Browning Biography," *The Nineteenth Century and After,* LXVIII (1910), 1072.

and the Book she found "the strongest evidence that our great poet, broad-minded in many directions, . . . simply shared the widespread ignorance which Catholics have almost hopelessly to contend with."[79] To illustrate her charge, Miss Hickey cited examples from *The Ring and the Book,* including the Caponsacchi-Pompilia relationship and the final speech by the Pope. In both cases she accused the poet of failing to recognize the incongruity of the incidents, the spirit behind them, and their absolute incompatibility with Roman Catholicism.[80] She concluded not that Browning was intellectually dishonest, but that he was intellectually incompetent to speak fairly of matters concerning the Roman Catholic church and that, despite his ignorance, he insisted on speaking. Browning, she wrote, "sees only with the eyes of a stranger, and whatever utterances he may give to his *dramatis personae,* are not the utterances of one who, like Chaucer and Shakespeare, knows all and understands all."[81]

Henry Jones, who was not wholly unfavorable to the poet, disliked the poet's view of knowledge. Browning's radical rejection of knowledge involves, according to Jones, "a fatal inconsistency here between his agnosticism and his optimism which no dialectical skill on the part of the poet . . . could finally overcome."[82]

The two adverse comments from 1910 yet to be reported— those by Leslie Stephen and Gamaliel Bradford, Jr.—were suggestive rather than specific. In discussing Browning's much-

[79]*Ibid.*

[80]*Ibid.,* p. 1073. DeVane (*Handbook,* pp. 334–335) calls the theology put into the Pope's mouth "an anachronism," but attempts to defend it on the grounds that it is "good theology" and "Browning's reading of life." This is not, however, nor is meant to be, an answer to the objections raised by Miss Hickey.

[81]*Ibid.,* p. 1073.

[82]*Idealism as a Practical Creed* (Glasgow, 1910), p. 184. For earlier comments by Jones, see above, pp. 17–20.

talked-about obscurity Bradford hinted that perhaps the poet's "perversity in the choice of form covers a greater inadequacy in matter than we might at first suppose."[83] Objecting to the frequent difficulty of Browning's style, he continued that "one is inclined to suspect that if he had had deep things to say, he would have said them simply. It so often happens so. Can it be possible that the poetic medium served his purpose, after all, where prose would have betrayed him?"[84] Bradford's criticism, however, suffers because he did not illustrate his point specifically.

Leslie Stephen's remark that certain of Browning's poems "contain discussions of metaphysical problems . . . but can scarcely be regarded as successful either poetically or philosophically"[85] constitutes a criticism only of the poetry of Browning's later years, but it deserves notice here, not because it casts fresh light upon Browning's thought, but because it has reappeared in each edition of *The Encyclopaedia Britannica* from the time of its original inclusion through 1954.

As we can see from comparing the volume of their writings with the mass produced by Browning's supporters during the centenary observation, the adverse critics make a pretty poor show in 1912. For sheer bravery, however, no one surpassed William Norman Guthrie, for he voiced his complaint in the face of the New York Browning Society, gathered for the sole purpose of honoring Browning on the occasion of the centennial. In a good-humored address, Guthrie told his audience that too many people have been led to think that because Browning was a great poet he was also a great thinker, teacher, and philosopher; and that there is "no reason to be-

[83]Gamaliel Bradford, Jr., "Browning and Saint-Beuve," *North American Review*, CXCI (1910), 492.

[84]*Ibid.*, p. 492.

[85]"Robert Browning," *The Encyclopaedia Britannica* (1910 ed.), IV, 673.

lieve that his doctrine of God is truer than that of Josiah Royce or Theodore Roosevelt."[86] Making his point even clearer, he argued:

> The thinking of Browning, then, is no more or less than the thinking of a certain type of man who happens to be a poet. ... Browning's only message, if message he has, that is authoritative for other men besides, is to be found in his artistic contribution to the world. It is rather what he *did* that counts, than what he *said*. Rather what he created than what he believed or thought. It is time that we should cease quoting men solemnly with an authority taken surreptitiously from one field to another. The power of a name should not be invoked outside the sphere of its relevancy.[87]

Unfortunately for the adverse critics, Guthrie did not develop this topic at length, but returned to the subject of his talk, "Browning and the Drama."

Percy Lubbock's attack was even more severe and was based upon a condemnation of Browning's belief that the value of the struggle is in the struggle itself and that consequently the struggle is more important than the end. Just as Browning accepted this doctrine of the struggle in life, wrote Lubbock,

> So in the world of ideas his delight was in the process itself, in the mercurial dance of thought, till thought will accept no other fulfillment than to go dancing on for ever. Thus Browning could be satisfied with the self-stultifying conclusion that energy was its own end and conflict its own eternal reward. He could celebrate the antagonism between good and evil without caring for the implication that, if it is the fight itself

[86]William Norman Guthrie, "Browning and the Drama," *NYBS Addresses,* pp. 51–52.
[87]*Ibid.,* p. 52.

which is the one essential, the names of the antagonists could be exchanged without spoiling the moral.[88]

On one point at least Lubbock was too sanguine, for he wrote that "a point already so freely conceded as that Browning was no philosopher need not be further laboured."[89] As we have already seen in this chapter, and as we shall see again in the next, Lubbock's remark was more than a little premature.

The adverse criticism after this time was sparse indeed, and one could almost imagine that the flood of favorable criticisms in 1912 had drowned out all other voices. Nevertheless, these voices were audible, if weak. They may be represented by Dixon Scott's chapter on Browning in his *Men of Letters* (1916) and by the random remarks of Albert Mordell in his book *The Erotic Motive in Literature* (1919). Browning's optimism displeased Mordell, especially as it found expression in *Rabbi Ben Ezra*. This happy view of old age he called a matter of wishful and unsound thinking, an argument that "One might as well pretend that old age was the better part of life, and one would then possibly be able to enjoy it."[90]

Dixon Scott saw much to admire in Browning as a poet, but was sure that the title of philosopher is ill-fitting. Calling Browning a "homely" poet because of his realism, his interest in common things, and his potential as a source of interest for the common man, he continued:

> It is plain, to begin with, that it was this practical attitude towards poetry, continued in his later work, that both gained him his intimidating title of philosopher and robbed him of any real right to it. He was no true speculator, in spite of his

[88]"Robert Browning," *The Quarterly Review,* CCXVII (1912), 441.
[89]*Ibid.,* p. 444.
[90]*The Erotic Motive in Literature* (New York, 1919), p. 85.

followers: ... Long before Harvard had invented the word he was only a pragmatist. His Rabbi Ben Ezras and Blougrams and Karshish are all agents acting on his behalf, sent out to find him the Elixir if he can. Far more a physician than a metaphysician, he delights in discussing the problems of the body, and sees the soul as a superior drug or stimulus, a medicine for the man who encloses it—not greatly different in character from the large restoratives of arts or gems or seas.[91]

Scott's simultaneous admiration for Browning's poetry and displeasure with those who insist on making a philosopher of him are displayed when the writer laughs at the "Dear, queer, estimable people! 'Does Browning urge this?' they ask; and 'Did he mean us to regard the other?'; and go gathering maxims in his poems—gleaning fossils in a field of corn and poppies. How much they would have us miss!"[92]

On the whole then, we can say that the years 1910–1919 dealt kindly with Browning's reputation as a thinker. The adverse critics were at their strongest from 1910 to 1912, but the favorable voices were even stronger; and, if both sides were too tired after the centennial exertions to say much more, it must be admitted that the cries of the adverse critics were the first to die down, not to be raised loud again, as we shall see, until the middle of the next decade.

[91]Dixon Scott, "The Homeliness of Browning," *Men of Letters* (London, 1916), pp. 251–252.
[92]*Ibid.,* p. 254.

The Browning Society, I need not say, as well as Browning himself, are fair game for criticism. . . . and, as Wilkes was no Wilkeite, I am quite other than a Browningite.

⊘ BROWNING TO EDMUND YATES

A REACTION

ALTHOUGH THE 1920'S WERE TO SEE the battle lines for and against Browning pretty sharply drawn, there were a considerable number of writers who took a temperate view of Browning the thinker. Some of these authors found both merits and faults in his "philosophical" poems, others attributed his reputation as a thinker to misguided zealousness of the Browning Societies, and still others contented themselves with moderate statements, arguing neither side.

An essay by C. T. Winchester typifies the middle-of-the-road attitude. Avoiding any direct judgment of the poet's thought, Winchester interpreted the method by which Browning attempted to solve his philosophic problems, a method which assumes "that our unsophisticated, spontaneous affections are a safer guide to happiness than prudence or ambition."[1] Prudence and ambition, however, are later equated with methodical thought, which Winchester judged lacking in Browning's poetry because Browning "is impatient to be at the goal of his argument; he starts a thought and leaves it half unuttered to hasten after another."[2] The restlessness of Browning's mind is again pointed out, this time with a

[1]"Browning: General Characteristics," *An Old Castle and Other Essays* (New York, 1922), p. 298.
[2]*Ibid.*, p. 306.

71

fleeting and perhaps uncomplimentary reference to Tennyson. According to Winchester, Browning's mind

> is always a-wrestle. It never lies quiet to mirror the shapes of passing thought, as Tennyson's always does. Still less can he endure the reasoning process. He cannot delay for the deliberate steps of logic. You will find all Browning's deepest beliefs rest at last not on reasoning but on the swifter assurance of intuition.[3]

The care with which Winchester phrased himself is noteworthy. It is not immediately apparent whether or not he approved Browning's thought processes. The fact that Browning did not arrange his thoughts methodically does not necessarily imply that he had not worked them out methodically. It might as well imply that Browning's thought had been too swift to find full expression in his poetry. On the other hand, one cannot assume that, in the phrase "the swifter assurances of intuition," Winchester held a belief that this speedy method of evading the reasoning process is superior to that process.

Other types of moderate estimates of Browning during the Twenties can be illustrated by four diverse examples: Arthur Compton-Rickett's *Robert Browning: Humanist,*[4] Louis Cazamian's *L'Évolution Psychologique et la Litterature en Angleterre (1660–1914),*[5] Henry Van Dyke's "The Glory of the Imperfect: Robert Browning's Poetry,"[6] and Paul de Reul's "The Art and Thought of Robert Browning."[7]

Because they are quite brief, Cazamian's comments can be dealt with first. Of Browning's work, he wrote: "La recherche de la vérité philosophique ou morale, la solution

[3]*Ibid.,* p. 308.
[4]New York, 1925.
[5]Paris, 1920.
[6]*Companionable Books* (New York, 1924), pp. 235–287.
[7]*Rice Institute Pamphlet,* XIII (1926), 227–304. In a later revision (Bruxelles, 1929) this became *L'Art et la Pensée de Robert Browning.*

d'un conflit entre les aspects divers du vrai ou du bien, tel est l'objet que Browning se propose d'ordinaire en écrivant."[8] No judgment was passed, however, upon the success or failure of Browning's ventures in search of philosophic or moral truth. The French scholar, like Winchester, had merely made a statement of fact. Nor does his later observation that Browning's concern with rationalism and argumentation is reminiscent of that same concern in the neoclassical period help us to place Cazamian on one side or the other in the controversy over Browning as a thinker.[9]

Compton-Rickett's references to Browning's thought likewise are oblique, for he wished to point out characteristics of the poet that were humanistic in nature. As a result, other aspects of Browning's verse were played down in deference to these traits, as is indicated here: "To my mind, the humanist Browning seems of much larger significance than the theological or merely didactic Browning."[10] Although the purpose of this statement was to exalt Browning's humanism, an implicit judgment is delivered upon his theology and his teaching.

Of Browning's utterances on religion, Compton-Rickett remarked that "What used to be called the 'message of Browning,' his religious speculations and moral disputations no longer stir a lively interest. But this side of Browning always seemed to me exaggerated out of all proportion."[11] Further, the critic noted, when Browning

> speaks to us of his own convictions, as we find he is doing in the thin disguise of *Abt Vogler* or *Rabbi Ben Ezra,* or without any disguise in *Reverie and Prospice*—he speaks as a sturdy moralist rather than as a spiritual seer.[12]

[8]Cazamian, p. 213.
[9]*Ibid.,* p. 214.
[10]Compton-Rickett, p. 25.
[11]*Ibid.,* p. 17.
[12]*Ibid.,* p. 51.

Lastly, the claims of Dean Inge to the contrary notwith-
standing,[13] he found "very little mysticism in Browning."[14]
In such statements there is no attempt either to praise or to
denigrate the poet's thought.

In his lengthy essay "The Glory of the Imperfect: Robert
Browning's Poetry," Henry Van Dyke, in addition to describing in some detail Browning's doctrine of imperfection,
made a number of observations which are pertinent to the
picture of Browning's reputation in the Twenties. On the
one hand, Van Dyke could be complimentary, as when he
wrote that "The clew to Browning's mind . . . is vivid and
inexhaustible curiosity, dominated by a strangely steady optimism."[15] Again, in Browning's treatment of the Incarnation,
Van Dyke discovered "the religious message that the world
most needs to-day."[16] Nevertheless, Van Dyke plainly did not
share the enthusiasm of the Browning Societies. His distinction is clear:

> It is a mistake to say that Browning is a metaphysical poet;
> he is a psychological poet. His interest does not lie in the
> abstract problems of time and space, mind and matter, di-
> vinity and humanity. It lies in the concrete problems of op-
> portunity and crisis, flesh and spirit, man the individual and
> God the person.[17]

Having made his distinction, and having praised Browning's faith in God and his teaching of the Incarnation, Van
Dyke proceeded to indicate two fallacies in the poet's thought,
both grounded in his attempt to leave the realm of the concrete and the psychological for that of the abstract and the

[13]See pp. 27–28 for Dean Inge's remarks.
[14]Compton-Rickett, p. 49.
[15]Van Dyke, p. 246.
[16]*Ibid.*, p. 280.
[17]*Ibid.*, p. 257. Along the same lines, Van Dyke writes (p. 256) that
"His topic is not the soul, in the abstract, but souls in the concrete."

philosophical. One of these weaknesses is Browning's view of life as a continuous struggle, in which effort is all important; the second is Browning's conception of the problem of good and evil. Of the former, Van Dyke wrote:

> ... it is in the working out of this doctrine into an ethical system that Browning enters upon dangerous ground, and arrives at results which seem to obscure the clearness, and to threaten the stability of the moral order, by which alone, the ultimate good of humanity can be attained. Here, it seems to me, his teaching, especially in its later utterances, is often confused, turbulent, misleading. His light is mixed with darkness. He seems almost to say that it matters little which way we go, provided only we go.[18]

Continuing in this vein, Van Dyke added that Browning undervalued discipline and self-restraint and placed too much emphasis upon activity and passion.

Van Dyke's adverse criticism of Browning's view of good and evil is directed at the poet's belief in the illusoriness of evil. "Browning," he complained, "was at times misled by a perilous philosophy into a position where the vital distinction between good and evil dissolved away in a cloud of unreality."[19] Because of this failure to distinguish clearly good from evil in *Ferishtah's Fancies* and the *Parleyings,* Van Dyke warned that the reader of these volumes "will find himself in a nebulous moral world for the supposed necessity of showing that evil is always a means to good tempts to the assertion that it has no other reality."[20] This line is extended in Van Dyke's statement that

> Effort, struggle, noble conflict would be impossible in a world where there were no moral certainties or realities, but all men

[18]*Ibid.,* pp. 281–282.
[19]*Ibid.,* p. 284.
[20]*Ibid.,* p. 285.

felt that they were playing at a stupid game like the Caucus
race in *Alice in Wonderland,* where everything went round
in a circle and every runner received a prize.[21]

Van Dyke's conclusion, however, was that the merits of
Browning's message outweighed the deficiencies of his philosophy: "True, the prophecy is not complete. But it is inspiring."[22]

Another middle-of-the-road estimate of Browning's achievement as a thinker is Paul de Reul's "The Art and Thought of
Robert Browning," published in 1926. M. de Reul had been
lecturing in America on Browning, but he had begun to
suspect that the poet's admirers had concerned themselves
overmuch with Browning the teacher.[23] He singled out for
special criticism Henry Jones and John Bury, both of whom,
he felt, had "too much Hegelianized our poet."[24] He declared
Browning's philosophy to be the result of a struggle between
pantheism and individualism.[25] Like his philosophy, Browning's
religion he called "a reasonable Christianity . . . a compromise, a true Victorian compromise between his philosophy
or his reason and the religion of his first education."[26] In
other words, the influence of Browning's fundamentalist upbringing was somehow merged with his own conclusions about
man's relationship to his Maker.

Although de Reul was not on the whole unfriendly to
Browning, he did indicate three aspects of Browning's thought
that seemed to him to be weak. The first is that in postulat-
ing the existence of God and soul, Browning has suffered a
lapse from logical thinking. According to the lecturer,

[21]*Ibid.,* pp. 285–286.
[22]*Ibid.,* p. 286.
[23]De Reul, p. 230.
[24]*Ibid.,* p. 275.
[25]*Ibid.,* p. 277.
[26]*Ibid.,* pp. 281–282.

He says: to know that I do not know something is an interesting fact—and, trespassing beyond logic, he adds: and
proves that the something exists:

> "Fact it is I know I know not something which is fact as
> much." He boldly applies the same reasoning to his two postu-
> lates, God and Soul. . . . But Browning happily corrects his rea-
> soning by saying that it is valid only for himself (proves them
> such for me). In other words, he improves the "ontological
> proof" by basing it on a personal religious experience.[27]

The poet's statements about immortality, especially those advanced in *La Saisiaz,* also disturbed de Reul, who wrote:

> There is no reason to give him especial praise for the doctrine
> laid down in *La Saisiaz,* for it is not necessarily the highest
> morally and it deprives his poetry of some noble sources of
> inspiration. . . . He is stayed in his lyrical flights, his wings
> being bound by his individualism. He is the captive of it. It
> biases his ideas of immortality. It also hampers his outlook on
> the universe, and the expression of his pantheistic feeling.[28]

Further, de Reul claimed that the poet placed too much
emphasis upon Eros, doing disservice to unmarried people
and presenting a faulty moral teaching.[29] Along the same
lines, de Reul objected to Browning's attitude toward love:

> . . . I will not admit that only by love, that is to say by sex,
> can our souls be saved, and this is very nearly the gist of the
> passage in Cristina where the man who speaks, if not Brown-
> ing, has at least all of Browning's sympathy:

> > "Doubt you if, in some such moment,
> >   As she fixed me she felt clearly,

[27]*Ibid.,* p. 278.
[28]*Ibid.,* p. 292.
[29]*Ibid.,* pp. 296–297.

Ages past the soul existed,
Here an age 'tis resting merely,
And hence fleets again for ages,
While the true end, sole and single,
It stops here for is, this love-way,
With some other soul to mingle?
Else it loses what it lived for,
And eternally must lose it;
Better ends may be in prospect,
Deeper blisses (if you choose it),
But this life's end and this love-bliss
Have been lost here."[30]

David Loth, in his book on the Brownings (1929), was less concerned directly with Browning's thought than with those who had created and fostered Browning's reputation as a thinker. Arguing that they had "insured for him the apprehensive, deliberate neglect of casual readers,"[31] he wrote:

The disciples agreed on only one thing, that Robert Browning was a great philosopher. They were quite wrong, for they confused scholarship with philosophy. Browning was a poet ... and he used the philosophies of other men as a matter of course without even subscribing to them himself, much less originating them. If he ever had a strictly new thought of a kind to qualify him as a philosopher, he kept it to himself, and he was not a man to practice that sort of intellectual reticence. It is safe to say that every time he was called a philosopher he was libeled.[32]

Loth's view that the critics ought to have distinguished between the poet and the poet-philosopher created by the "disciples" of Browning was not wholly subscribed to by D. C.

[30]*Ibid.*, p. 296.
[31]David Loth, *The Brownings: A Victorian Idyll* (New York, 1929), p. 278.
[32]*Ibid.*, p. 274.

Somervell, who in 1929 published two items of interest to this study. Somervell recalled that to his generation Browning had been important both as a thinker and as a religious teacher because "he strengthened in many readers the faith that he did not himself possess."[33] Concerning the poet's conclusions about immortality, Somervell commented that "Optimism convinces him of Heaven, but his furious energy will allow no harps and haloes there. . . . Even a Benthamite utilitarian might be willing to accept a Heaven in which he could still find bustle and 'progress.' "[34]

It is, however, in his essay "The Reputation of Robert Browning" that Somervell showed how far different his moderate view was from that of Loth, who had attributed the poet's fame as a philosopher almost exclusively to the Browning enthusiasts. The blame, Somervell implied, must be shared both by Browning and his followers:

> And lastly there is Browning's "message," his "philosophical and religious teaching," and all those things about which so much used reverently to be said; . . . Well, the Victorian age was a very curious period of history. . . . among the Victorian "documents" the "teaching" of Robert Browning is likely to occupy a place, if only because that teaching was in fact so eagerly welcomed in his own day.
>
> Still, as Mr. F. L. Lucas has said,[35] that teaching interposes a barrier between us and the poetry which was made its vehicle. It is a pity; and if it is partly our fault, no doubt it is partly Browning's fault also.[36]

The words "about which so much used reverently to be said,"

[33]*English Thought in the Nineteenth Century* (London, 1929), p. 165.

[34]*Ibid.*, p. 166.

[35]*New Statesman*, XXXII (1928), 157.

[36]D. C. Somervell, "The Reputation of Robert Browning," *Essays and Studies by Members of the English Association*, XV (1929), 137–138.

coming at the close of the Twenties from the pen of one who was trying to assess Browning's general reputation, are as important to this study as is Somervell's implied judgment of Browning's thought, for they indicate that—from Somervell's observations, at least—Browning's thought was getting less, or at any rate less reverent, attention that it had once attracted.

Had Somervell written his article five years earlier, he might very well have modified his statement, for the first five years of the Twenties saw published a great amount of praise for Browning as a thinker. Certain of these compliments were very slight, consisting of a commendatory word or two on minor aspects of Browning's thought. For example, Israel Abrahams, in his *By-Paths in Hebraic Bookland,* was pleased to find that Browning had recognized "certain elements of absolute truth" in Judaism and was even more pleased that the poet had been possessed of the good sense to present these bits of truth through such Jewish *dramatis personae* as Ben Karshook and Rabbi Ben Ezra.[37] Another example of this sort is R. L. Megroz' claim that Browning's understanding of the workings of the human mind was so great that in *Bishop Blougram's Apology* he gave an excellent description of "infantile regression of thought."[38]

The criticism of the early Twenties did not, of course, neglect the larger elements of Browning's thought. In her *Browning Critiques* (1921) Margret Holmes Bates took pains to defend the poet both from those who had attacked his optimism and from those who had praised it. She held that Browning was not at all a Christian theist, looking forward with strong hope and vibrant faith to a future life, but rather that he was better represented by the poem *A Bean-Stripe,*

[37]"Browning's 'Ben Karshook,' " *By-Paths in Hebraic Bookland* (Philadelphia, 1920), p. 275.

[38]*Walter de la Mare: A Biographical and Critical Study* (London, 1924), p. 116.

with "its sound philosophy, and fascinating turn of argument."[39] She wrote:

> Many students of Browning see in this widely read man, this philosophic, analytic thinker, not the indifference, the unconcern for the future, that all profound students must arrive at soon or late, but they interpret his content in the present, his careless view of the future, as *Christian Faith.*
> Nothing of this faith is to be found in his poems, either early or late. He studied all religions and subscribed wholly to none.[40]

Many of Browning's followers would probably have rejected for him the support of Mrs. Bates, for most of them saw in Browning the eminent defender of Christianity. It is, for example, exceedingly difficult to reconcile her opinion of Browning's religion with that of C. T. Winchester, who, while remarking that Browning "sometimes seems a little over-indulgent of passion and impulse,"[41] could call Browning

> ... the most prominently and positively Christian poet of the last generation. And this is not principally because he was an avowed believer in some formulated creed—though he was gratifyingly orthodox in that direction, a good Presbyterian deacon of the Scotch Free Church in Florence and passing about the plate for the alms every Sunday—but I call him our great Christian poet rather because he held all his life, in spite of all the doubts and questionings of his age—of which he was by no means ignorant—a healthy, robust, hopeful faith in the great essentials of Christianity. . . . Browning's faith was based not so much upon externals or historical evidence as upon a

[39]Margret Holmes Bates, *Browning Critiques* (Chicago, 1921), p. 269.

[40]*Ibid.*, pp. 7–8.

[41]"Art, Love, and Religion in the Poetry of Robert Browning," *An Old Castle and Other Essays,* p. 346.

profound internal conviction of the fitness of the Christian
revelation to our deepest needs.[42]

Thus in 1922 Browning could be praised for his Christian
faith, whereas a year earlier he had been praised for his lack
of it.

On one other matter, that of logic, Winchester touched. As
though in answer to Santayana, he denied that Browning
fell "into the error of claiming that the desire for immortality
is itself proof enough of immortality."[43] On the contrary,
Browning's faith came into play at this point: "Nay [wrote
Winchester] God has revealed it, says the Christian [Brown-
ing, apparently], and the heart God hath made leaps to
accept the revelation God hath given."[44] Although Winchester emphasized Browning's faith,[45] it is obvious that he
much admired the poet's mind.

Praise of a different sort was accorded Browning's mind
in Lafcadio Hearn's "Studies in Browning," published in
1922. Hearn's comments have for this study the added interest of having been originally the substance of his lectures
at the University of Tokyo. In the simple language he used
to communicate his thoughts to the Japanese students Hearn
emphasized this point: that Browning was not primarily or
even very often a philosophic poet,[46] but that the philosophy
to which he did adhere was "an optimistic pantheism, in-
culcating effort as the very first and highest duty of life."[47]

[42]*Ibid.*, pp. 352–353.
[43]Winchester, p. 355.
[44]*Ibid.*
[45]See, for example, pp. 356–361.
[46]Examples: "But you must not suppose that Browning lives much
in the regions of abstract philosophy" (p. 199) ; "But Browning is
not especially a philosophical poet. We find his philosophy flashing out
only at long intervals" (p. 173). *Appreciations of Poetry*, ed. John
Erskine (London, 1922).
[47]*Ibid.*, pp. 172–173.

Further, Hearn termed Browning's moral teachings "mostly larger than the teachings of any creed."[48]

Unlike Hearn, however, certain other commentators were not so careful as he had been to qualify his statements about Browning's philosophy. In the following two years three writers—Emma J. Burt, Rufus N. Jones, and Frances M. Sim[49]—praised him both as a thinker and as a mystic.

In her book *The Seen and Unseen in Browning,* Emma J. Burt showed quite plainly her admiration for Browning's thinking and frequently mentioned it in connection with the term *mystic* and its cognates. Quoting Inge to support her contention, she warned the reader that "it must be kept in mind that he is not only a dramatic poet, but also a mystic."[50] Again: "Robert Browning, as we well know, was a deep thinker and the mysteries of man's origin had an immense interest for him. His was that strong and adventurous spirit which ever strives to reach the Truth."[51] In the same vein she wrote:

> Browning as a mystical thinker seldom lets us lose sight of that intangible mysterious inner vision which is the property of the seer. If it is not always possible to follow him in the inwardness of his thought, neither is it altogether possible to escape the consciousness of its invisible presence.[52]

Perhaps more outspoken was Rufus Jones, in his article, "Mysticism in Robert Browning," which appeared in 1923 in *The Biblical Review.* To Jones, Browning represented a new

[48]*Ibid.,* p. 195.

[49]Emma J. Burt, *The Seen and Unseen in Browning* (Oxford, 1923) ; Rufus M. Jones, "Mysticism in Robert Browning," *The Biblical Review,* VIII (1923), 229–245 ; Frances M. Sim, *Robert Browning: Poet and Philosopher, 1850–1889* (New York, 1924).

[50]Burt, pp. 40–41.

[51]*Ibid.,* p. 185.

[52]*Ibid.,* p. 77.

mysticism and a few faith that "rested upon a seasoned philosophy which he held."[53] "His was a mysticism," said Jones, "of the best affirmation type, which after centuries of intellectual and spiritual travail has found a better way than the *via negativa*. . . . This new mysticism builds solidly upon the normal experiences of man's soul."[54] Jones explained his terms:

> But when Browning says, "feel Him," and exalts that method of approach in place of slow and painful rationalization, he is not setting emotions over against reason, as a better source of knowledge. He is insisting upon the great fact that the spirit of man, in its unified and total being, can partake of God and does discover that His spirit presses palpitatingly over and around ours.
>
> > "Rejoice, we are allied
> > To that which doth provide.
> > . . . .
> > "Nearer we hold of God
> > Who gives than of His tribes that take."
> > > (*Rabbi Ben Ezra*)
>
> That is precisely what the sane affirmative mystic means by mysticism. God and man are allied, are kin.[55]

It seems almost as though Jones was hailing Browning as the prophet of a new cult—affirmative mysticism—in which every man can be a mystic simply by proclaiming a joyful acceptance of life.

A similar connection between Browning's philosophy and mysticism was made by Frances M. Sim in her *Robert Brown-*

[53]Jones, p. 230.
[54]*Ibid.*, pp. 233–234.
[55]*Ibid.*, p. 235. It is interesting to speculate what damage this sort of thing has done to Browning's reputation.

ing: Poet and Philosopher, 1850–1889 (1924), a book whose title promised far more than its contents fulfilled.[56] Writing of *Christmas-Eve,* she said:

> In this poem and many others of the middle period of Browning's life the Christian mystic in the poet clothed itself. Upon that philosophy of the practical mystic the poet rose to his highest in "Saul," "The Epistle of Karshish the Arab Physician," "A Death in the Desert," "Fears and Scruples," "Cristina"; in the two great landmarks of Browning philosophy—"Abt Vogler" and "Rabbi Ben Ezra"; and the intellectualist's delight—"A Grammarian's Funeral."[57]

Deeper than this Mrs. Sim did not delve. Having made Browning a proponent of practical mysticism, she contented herself with such comments as the following: " 'Wholly distrust thy reason,' is Browning's advice in difficulty";[58] and "The sense of incompleteness is man's salvation, says Browning, as well as his misery."[59]

C. N. Wenger's *The Aesthetics of Robert Browning* (1924) was more carefully done. Having at first—somewhat like Hearn—warned the readers that Browning "had no system, but only a scattered and poetical use of ideas concerning God, Man, and the external Universe,"[60] Wenger proceeded to examine cautiously certain of Browning's individual be-

[56]This book, despite its title, is worthless to this study, for it is merely a string of quotations and paraphrases of Browning's poems. William Lyon Phelps's comment on her *Robert Browning: The Poet and the Man, 1833–1846* (New York, 1923 ed.) is nearly appropriate here. He wrote: "I have read many inaccurate and silly books on Browning, but this outclasses them all." *As I Like It, Second Series* (New York, 1924), p. 18.

[57]Frances M. Sim, *Robert Browning: Poet and Philosopher, 1850–1889,* p. 14.

[58]*Ibid.,* p. 167.

[59]*Ibid.,* p. 204.

[60]*The Aesthetics of Robert Browning* (Ann Arbor, 1924), p. 39.

liefs, always keeping before the reader's mind the fact that Browning believed truth to be an "intuitive sort of knowledge"[61]—that is, knowledge attained through the senses, the intuition, or by other than strictly rational means. To Wenger's mind, Browning saw God as "not at all susceptible of proof, or as unprovable by ordinary means, at any rate . . ."[62] and love as the nearest perfect of all experiences in life, represented in his poetry "as a reduction of the essence of all things to emotional activity."[63]

In an examination of Browning's treatment of this emotional activity, Wenger found occasion for both agreement and disagreement with critics like Santayana. First, he insisted that those who complain of Browning's giving too high a place to the emotions have not considered well enough the fact that Browning shows high regard for "intuitive knowledge" and that, after all, "he insists continually upon the relativity of all the materials of life, love included with the others."[64] In other words, Browning was an absolute relativist in that he could, when pushed for a rational explanation of his propositions, fall back upon the position that they were valid only for himself. Wenger felt that

> The just criticism of Browning at this point is that he overstresses the relativity of the materials of life. He says that "The prize is in the process," and this is to leave knowledge, power, and love in constant flux without stopping places ever or anywhere from which to contemplate and judge whether the process is a worth-while "prize," or whether the direction of its process is one worthy of continuance.[65]

To Browning "progress is . . . both the means and the end"

[61]*Ibid.*, p. 56. Wenger does not attempt to judge whether it is justifiable or possible to erect a philosophy on intuitional grounds.
[62]*Ibid.*, p. 45.
[63]*Ibid.*, p. 57.
[64]Wenger, p. 59.
[65]*Ibid.*

of life and the fact that man can choose this philosophy of progress is "a sufficient judgment of its process and direction."[66] "And it is too," remarked Wenger in partial judgment, "in many ways, a quite satisfactory principle whereby at once to explain the universe and to live in accordance with the explanation."[67]

G. H. Bonner's remarks on Browning were far more enthusiastic than those of most of the poet's admirers. A few sample statements will indicate the burden of this article, which appeared in 1924. An early comment that Browning "is poet, philosopher, historian, and novelist, all in one"[68] set the theme of this essay. Moreover, continued Bonner, "Because Browning, like Plato and Dante, has reached this eternal and immutable truth, and because he has clothed it in words and images of no less eternal beauty, his work will endure."[69] And that Bonner was perfectly convinced that Browning combined the philosophic mind of Plato with the poetic fire of Dante is clear from the high spot of the essay:

> What philosophy is there in *Christmas Eve,* a philosophy that, once accepted, would settle for ever all the strife and bitterness of warring religious sects.
> But it is when philosophy and music are wedded, as in *Evelyn Hope,* that Browning reaches his most sublime heights ...we may read it a dozen times without realising the profundity of the thought which it contains; ... As we meditate upon this poem the vistas which it opens out grow more stupendous and "Love the Unconquerable" becomes something more than a phrase.[70]

If this plethora of statements favorable to Browning's

[66]*Ibid.,* pp. 62–64.
[67]*Ibid.,* p. 64.
[68]G. H. Bonner, "Robert Browning," *The Nineteenth Century and After,* XCVI (1924), 223.
[69]*Ibid.,* p. 227.
[70]*Ibid.,* p. 221.

thought had continued beyond the mid-point of the Twenties, Somervell would have been unable to note a lack of interest in Browning's philosophy. But for some reason there was comparatively little material published during the last five years of the decade in praise of Browning as a thinker. Further, the statements which followed 1925 were somehow less exuberant than some of those already treated in this chapter. As instances of the favorable criticism of the late Twenties, let us examine the statements of only three representative essayists—Penrhyn Chave, Watson Kirkconnell, and Anthony Crossley.

Kirkconnell's article is devoted to a discussion of the *Epilogue* to *Dramatis Personae,* and the writer's praise is implicit in his interpretation of what Browning's poem has to say to the "sceptic liberal":

> ...that a calm survey of this universe does not wipe out the conception of God given us by Christ. For God is incarnate, potentially, in all mankind, and as man develops, the nature of God, the ideal toward which he strives, becomes more and more evident through the evolving nature of humanity. The incomplete knowledge and faltering love of mankind are revelations of the complete knowledge and perfect love of God.[71]

Browning's concepts of imperfection and progress are thus praised by Kirkconnell for teaching the "sceptic liberals" that the Incarnation, though to them unacceptable in the God-Man Christ, is acceptable as God-in-the-germ in all men.

Penrhyn Chave's article, "Philosophy and Poetry," is somewhat akin to Kirkconnell's in that he too praises the poet for discovering connections between God and man. Where Kirkconnell found evolution the answer, however, Chave substituted what he thought was Browning's concept of the function of the artist:

[71]"The *Epilogue* to *Dramatis Personae,*" *MLN,* XLI (1926), 219.

Browning . . . believed that the poet provided that very truth which the philosopher sought elsewhere. The artist, in his eyes, had a very special mission, the very one in fact which the philosopher arrogated to himself, that of explaining the unseen in terms of the seen. . . . He was the link between God and man, illustrating at once divine intentions for man and human searchings after God.[72]

Thus Chave could find in Browning the poet who has linked art with philosophy, the man who has evolved towards divinity somewhat more rapidly than his fellows and who thereby becomes "the link between God and man."

The last favorable critic to be dealt with in this chapter is Anthony Crossley, whose article, "Browning as a Dramatic Poet and Prophet," appeared in 1928. Browning's probings into the human mind he judged "seldom obscure, . . . almost always profound."[73] "The essence of all his teachings," wrote Crossley, "and the germ of all his philosophy, is to be found in these lines from *The Ring and the Book*: 'Through such souls alone/God stooping shows sufficient of his light/For us in the dark to rise by. And I rise.' "[74] This expressed faith in God's goodness as it is displayed in mankind Crossley judged "the one entry that remained absolutely unsmudged in his philosophic catalogue."[75]

While the favorable criticism of Browning as a thinker, so heavy in the first half of the decade, dwindled fairly rapidly with the approach of the end of the Twenties, the unfavorable criticism on the other hand grew from a slow trickle in the early Twenties to the proportions of a steady stream by 1929. It would seem also that the objections to

[72]"Philosophy and Poetry," *The Contemporary Review*, CXXX (1926), 218.

[73]Anthony Crossley, "Browning as a Dramatic Poet and Prophet," *The Spectator*, CXLI (1928), 45.

[74]*Ibid.*, p. 46.

[75]*Ibid.*, p. 44.

Browning's thought in the earlier years were rather weak, oblique, or (with the exception of Mrs. Russell's) quite general in nature. It is as though the adverse critics were hesitant to venture into a field dominated by the poet's admirers.

The comments of George E. Woodberry, in his *Studies of a Litterateur,* might well serve as an example at this juncture. His point is that Browning's thought was mechanical:

> Browning has . . . obtained a certain command which makes it impossible for him to fall below a definite and high excellence in expression, and thus he is always both facile and sure; but, beyond that, he has also developed habits of reasoning, so that his intellect is a mold, and no matter what goes into it, always gives out the same form of thought. In other words, there is something fairly to be described as mechanical in his thinking as well as in his handling: there is an intellectual routine in his works—the hardened ossified form of what was once a fluid and vital art.[76]

Spearheaded by the writings of Frances Theresa Russell, the attack on Browning's thought increased in tempo and in intensity during the middle Twenties. Furthermore, those who detracted from the poet's reputation as a thinker during this period differed widely as to the scope, the force, and the focus of their criticisms. In fact, Mrs. Russell's criticisms alone covered a diversity of matters and were scattered over this middle period.

One of the tenets of Browning's philosophy that Mrs. Russell attacked was the poet's much-praised optimism. Tracing the history of his *Weltansicht* through his poetry, she concluded that Browning was not as optimistic as he had been made out to be: the solutions of the various crises in *Pippa Passes* she judged "sheer fantastic romanticism";[77] the lesson

[76]George E. Woodberry, "Late Victorian Verse: Browning, Swinburne, Tennyson," *Studies of a Litterateur* (New York, 1921), p. 42.
[77]Frances Theresa Russell, "The Pessimism of Robert Browning,"

of a more mature work, *The Ring and the Book,* she found totally unoptimistic, "the utter nothingness of human testimony and estimation";[78] lastly, of Browning's final views she wrote:

> Is not that final *Epilogue* the last word? Years before the poet had said: "I shall know, being old." Now that he is old, what does he know? Quite literally, he does not know what he is talking about; for his theme is himself and the portrait drawn is so subtly specious, mistaking as it does disposition for character and accomplishment, that it is invalidated as a trustworthy report.[79]

Her criticism expanded, then, to include both Browning and his followers, the latter because they have exalted him as a teacher of optimism and the former for having promoted a false optimism, fostered by an *"aes triplex* of happy environment, buoyant disposition, and naive theology."[80] Because he buried a natural pessimism[81] beneath a superficial optimism, she finds him guilty of poor teaching and writes that, like the

---

Sewanee Review, XXXII (1924), 73. Another writer, Osbert Burdett, found Browning's optimism somewhat labored. He writes: "The buoyancy of Browning and Meredith is self-confessedly an effort to stem the current that they oppose." *The Beardsley Period: An Essay in Perspective* (London, 1925), p. 32.

[78]*Ibid.,* p. 73.

[79]*Ibid.,* p. 74.

[80]*Ibid.,* p. 76.

[81]Indeed, she writes (p. 76) that his pessimism is the quality for which the present century will value him. Speaking directly to the poet she writes: "Not for your love of the garish day, of shawms and trumpets, of C major and the Mode Palestrina, do we welcome and speed you on, but for the wistful minor of your *Toccata,* the ineffable unfulfillment of your *Compagna,* your confession that our joy may be three parts pain and dearly bought at that with strain and throe, your recognition that this curse will come upon us—to see our idols perish." Significantly enough, when this essay was reprinted in *One Word More on Browning,* it bore the title, "His Saving Grace of Pessimism."

hearts of the poet's time, "our heart beats that it is good to live and learn; only we are beginning to be more concerned that we learn aright."[82]

Two of Mrs. Russell's articles, one appearing in 1924[83] and the other two years later,[84] dealt with Browning's treatment of love in *The Ring and the Book*. In both essays she accused Browning of mishandling facts deliberately, thus betraying an intellectual dishonesty. Of the "gold and alloy" metaphor she writes that Browning, "when he inquires if the fiction which makes fact be alive be not fact too, he again betrays his indifference to a line that must be drawn by any apostle of truth."[85] This point was put somewhat more strongly in the second essay:

> Now no one is going to object to the infusion of fancy or make a fuss about the sacrosanctity of facts. But the real truth and unfortunate fact is that the poet's fancy, once admitted, took to masquerading as what but the primal verity itself; ... what he did was to distort the essentials until he might have been sued for libel had not his victims been dead for a long time.[86]

But Frances Russell's criticism of Browning's intellectual powers was not always so damning as this charge of dishonesty might lead cne to expect. An overall view of her volume of essays, *One Word More on Browning* (1927), leaves one suspicious that the author took a generally pessimistic view of the achievements of human thought. She tended to see Browning's failure as a thinker both as another example of

[82]*Ibid.*, p. 77.

[83]"Gold and Alloy," *SP*, XXI (1924), 467–479.

[84]"One Word More," *The University of California Chronicle*, XXVIII (1926), 99–101.

[85]Russell, "Gold and Alloy," p. 468. See, however, A. G. Drachmann, "Alloy and Gold," *SP*, XXII (1925), 418, for another interpretation of the metaphor.

[86]Russell, "One Word More," p. 100.

man's intellectual frailty and as the triumph of the poet in him over the thinker. An illustration of the latter case is her comment upon Browning's too frequently allowing "belief to duplicate the costume of truth and masquerade as knowledge."[87] She wrote:

> That Browning was not proof against this subtle deception is proof that he was more poet than philosopher and no scientist at all. His inability to distinguish speculation from fact, his reliance on mysticism, his frank plea for illusion—these indicate the poet; but the poet has a philosophic vein, and therein finds the deductive method, proceeding from hypothesis back to skilfully selected data, very convenient.[88]

Again she exonerated Browning on the grounds that he is a poet, not a thinker, by saying, "He was no more of a metaphysical scholar than the rest of our poets, but like all poets he had a certain fondness for popular philosophizing."[89] Therefore, Browning is excused from attacks upon the validity of his philosophy, but only at the expense of being placed on an intellectual level with "the rest of our poets."

That Browning's philosophical failures were shared by more than the poets only is implied in Mrs. Russell's disagreement with Santayana, who had called the poet's system "truncated." Browning's serious thinking she described as "a replica of the numerous other pyramids with which the Sahara of human ignorance is pathetically populated. . . ."[90]

Herbert Read, in his *Reason and Romanticism* (1926), was not quite so willing as Frances Russell to attribute Browning's failure to a general failure of human thought. For him, Browning was a psychological rather than metaphysical poet and therefore merits no serious consideration as a thinker.

[87]Russell, *One Word More on Browning* (Stanford, 1927), p. 102.
[88]*Ibid.*, pp. 102–103.
[89]*Ibid.*, p. 106.
[90]*Ibid.*, p. 107.

The poet, he wrote, "was neither mystical nor metaphysical, and I am not sure that it would not be legitimate to say he was just wordy."[91]

Although William Clyde DeVane intended in his *Browning's Parleyings: the Autobiography of a Mind* (1927) primarily to trace the development of, and the influences upon, Browning's mind, it is inevitable that he should have passed some judgments upon the validity of certain of Browning's philosophic conclusions. DeVane's book is important also because it serves as an answer to critics who would insist that it is unfair to judge the poet as a thinker. In his prefatory remarks, DeVane noted that Browning "finally took philosophy as his main business of life. As his poetic inspiration declined, and the earnestness of his moral purpose increased, he came into the lists as a philosopher armed cap-a-pie."[92]

The "Parleying" which deals most directly with Browning as a thinker is that with Bernard de Mandeville, for here the poet "delivers a summary of his philosophy in his own person."[93] It is in Browning's insistence upon a beneficent God and a morally free man that DeVane differed strongly with the poet. For Browning, evil is illusory, but man cannot perceive its unreality. In order that man shall not know that evil is not real, Browning is forced to say, however, that man's intellect simply is too weak to know, that it is incapable of real knowledge. To quote DeVane: "Thus Browning preserved his optimism by casting aspersions on the validity of man's knowing faculty; . . . he insisted on the necessity of man's ignorance. His faith is thus ultimately blind, and he is an intellectual agnostic. . . ."[94]

It might be submitted at this point that Browning's ag-

[91]Herbert Read, *Reason and Romanticism: Essays in Literary Criticism* (London, 1926), p. 52.

[92]William Clyde DeVane, *Browning's Parleyings: The Autobiography of a Mind* (New Haven, 1927), p. xiii.

[93]*Ibid.*, p. 1.

[94]*Ibid.*, p. 34.

nosticism was the result of logical thought, but DeVane seemed not to think so. In his chapter "Parleying with Francis Furini" he wrote:

> It is easy to see that this theory of the worthlessness of human intelligence ends inevitably in absolute scepticism. All ends in a blank darkness, which nothing can illumine. Browning's reason for degrading the intellect is of course that it impeaches what he wishes to believe.[95]

The final sentence of the quotation is indeed a damaging one, for it indicates a belief that Browning did not follow truth wherever it led, but that he rejected truth when it conflicted with his own system.

The last two years of the decade found no abatement of the stream of adverse criticism. W. O. Raymond, writing on "Browning and the Higher Criticism," extended the line of thought set forth by DeVane, interpreting Browning's arguments for Christianity in the light of his rejection of knowledge acquired by the intellect. He wrote that "The clue to Browning's religious position lies in the recognition of the fact that with him . . . it is the function of the heart to 'melt the reason's colder part.' His gnosticism is primarily emotional."[96] Further, although he praised the soliloquy of the Pope in *The Ring and the Book* as "one of the greatest examples of constructive religious thought in nineteenth century poetry,"[97] he concluded that Browning's scepticism invalidated portions of his religious thought. "It is evident," remarked Raymond,

> that Browning's abnegation of reason continually sprains his

[95]*Ibid.*, p. 188. This subjective view of knowledge is expounded in some detail on pp. 187–193 in DeVane's book.

[96]W. O. Raymond, "Browning and the Higher Criticism," *PMLA,* XLIV (1929), 608.

[97]*Ibid.*, p. 607.

argument whenever he is dealing with the historical bases of Christianity. For, if the incidents of the gospel narrative are placed beyond the pale of reason, it is difficult to show how they possess objective validity. The vacillation of the poet's own point of view on this ground is a testimony to the unsoundness of his premises.[98]

Browning's philosophy did not fare better at the hands of H. J. C. Grierson or John Macy, both of whose comments were published in 1928. In his *Lyrical Poetry from Blake to Hardy*, the former made clear his belief that the modern critic who considers either Tennyson or Browning a philosophical poet is mistaken[99] and that the concept of "Browning as a great and solemn thinker has gone out with the Browning Societies...."[100]

Macy made the same point with somewhat greater force, adding that Browning would himself have rejected the philosophic laurels awarded him. Macy advised those who have "made him a moralist and prophet and philosopher and all things dignified and worthy" to re-read *The Statue and the Bust*, which, in the words of the critic, "is a direct challenge to founded virtue, a threnody on illicit love not realized, of lost youth and passion killed by the encroachments of time."[101]

Finally, in 1929 there appeared two articles which placed Browning's merits as a serious thinker quite low. Writing for *The English Journal*, Earl Daniels presented his own reactions and those of a class of his college students to the

[98]*Ibid.*, p. 610.

[99]Writes Grierson (p. 66), "But indeed, until we disengage ourselves from the impression of Tennyson and Browning as great philosophical poets, which was the conviction of their later admirers, we shall fail to do justice to what they both undoubtedly were—very great and cunning artists...."

[100]*Ibid.*, p. 79.

[101]"The Victorious Victorians," *The Bookman*, LXVII (1928), 542–547.

poet's philosophy.[102] Browning's concepts of love and eternity, reported Daniels, came in for particular criticism:

> ...his assurances of an ultimate eternity of love offered a conception of heaven bound in the end to become nothing but tiresome. His last rides together, life-in-love or love-in-life were all hollow and unreal. ... In the doctrine of the ecstatic moment, Browning, the philosopher, lost all philosophical standing with the clear thinking minds before me.[103]

Daniels added that, in particular, the moral of *The Statue and the Bust* "stood clearly out for the shallow thing it was. "[104] It seems likely that Daniels agreed fully with his students and that his own approach to Browning's poetry had helped to foster the students' distaste for the poet's philosophy.

G. R. Elliott's article, appearing in the *Sewanee Review*, condemned Browning's thought on the grounds that the poet's mind was essentially unfit for philosophic thought. "The Browningite," he wrote disdainfully,

> has wonderingly pointed out that by the age of twenty-three the poet had adopted in all its essentials the "philosophy" that runs, or twists through the whole fabric of his work. But patient time has more and more untwisted that philosophy and displayed its inadequacy. Nowadays the wonder must be, not that Browning adopted it so early, but that a man of his intelligence could cling to it so long.[105]

Commenting that Browning did not have a philosophical mind, Elliott continued: "... when turned upon the central principles of life, his critical intelligence became blunt; when

[102]Contrast this with Padelford's report of 1907.

[103]Earl Daniels, "The Younger Generation Reads Browning and Tennyson," *The English Journal*, XVIII (1929), 657.

[104]*Ibid.*, p. 658.

[105]G. R. Elliott, "Browning's Whitmanism," *Sewanee Review*, XXXVII (1929), 167.

turned upon his own favorite set of ideas, it lost its edge completely."[106] An example of this uncritical mind at work Elliott found in Browning's portrayal of character, charging that the poet "could not veraciously represent character, insofar as character means the bringing of temperament under any rational and ethical control. At its worst, his poetry tries to demonstrate, as in 'By the Fireside' and 'The Statue and the Bust,' that the effects of character can be obtained through sheer quantity of emotion."[107]

And worse was yet to come.

[106] *Ibid.*, p. 168.
[107] *Ibid.*, p. 170.

"We critics as sweeps out your chimbly!
Much soot to remove from your flue, sir!
Who spares coal in kitchen an't you, sir!
And neighbors complain it's no joke, sir!
—You ought to consume your own smoke, sir!"

❂ FROM PACCHIAROTTO

THE DEEPENING
GLOOM

ALTHOUGH THE FLOOD OF ADVERSE
criticism which brought the Twenties to a close did not fully
silence the supporters of Browning as a philosopher, it is a
matter of fact that the years 1930–1939 were not favorable to
his reputation as a thinker. The reaction, as we have seen, had
been setting in rapidly, and there was little in the temper of
the Thirties to encourage a revival of Browning's philosophy.
It is, perhaps, unfortunate that Browning's supporters had
so frequently exalted in Browning the virtue of optimism;
for the Thirties, with an air of disillusionment and an eco-
nomic depression, was hardly the period to welcome with
enthusiasm a man both sainted and damned for his optimism. There were, nevertheless, a few staunch supporters
of the poet, and these attempted to promote and to defend
his philosophy of life.

Perhaps chief among these supporters was A. J. Armstrong,
whose contribution to Browning's fame has consisted of far
more than a few published words of praise for the poet. At
this point, however, it is with these printed comments that
we are concerned. Armstrong's article, "Browning's Testament of Hope," appeared late in 1935 in *The Baylor Bulletin.*
It is quite obvious that the heavy criticism of Browning's

thought during the Twenties had had very little effect on Armstrong's views, for he wrote confidently that "Robert Browning has made the greatest contribution to the spread of optimism so that it may be considered his supreme gift to the world."[1] Such an outlook in the Thirties is indeed rare and prepares us somewhat for his next remark: "His thoughts were so profound, and his ideas so fundamental, that his vision penetrated the mysterious curtains which concealed the light from less gifted mortals and then he saw that all was well."[2] Finally, to this praise of Browning's optimism and his profundity is added a note of prophecy: "The time has come when the light of truth shall disperse the darkness and we raise our bowed heads to give thanks for the testament of hope of which a great poet has made us his beneficiaries."[3]

Armstrong was mistaken in assuming that the time for grateful acceptance of Browning's "testament of hope" had arrived, and there were few enough critics who would have agreed. Among these few, Miriam Allen de Ford and Charles Grosvenor Osgood might stand as representative, for both defended Browning from the attacks of the many who had complained that his was a shallow, ill-grounded optimism. "Perhaps," noted Mrs. de Ford, "the only thing which keeps Browning from being completely in accord with our later era is his ebullient and militant optimism."[4] However, she continued:

Browning's optimism is not the shallow philosophy of a Pollyanna. It is courage "in spite of hell and high water":

[1]"Browning's Testament of Hope," *The Baylor Bulletin,* XXXVIII (1935), 8. Mr. Armstrong's devotion to Browning was evident in his teaching, in the *Baylor Browning Interests* series, and in the fine Browningiana library he helped to establish at Baylor University.
[2]*Ibid.,* p. 9.
[3]*Ibid.,* p. 30.
[4]"Robert Browning," *British Authors of the Nineteenth Century,* eds. Stanley J. Kunitz and Howard Haycraft (New York, 1936), p. 88.

he is above all "one who never feared the future, but faced forward." Impulsive and violent as he often was—and what Browning himself was appears in his poetry in every line— he was steadfast always in that, always a yea-sayer to life.[5]

Akin to Mrs. de Ford's defense is Osgood's, whose comments were first published in 1935. Browning's was not, he insisted, a mere, blind optimism, for the poet was well aware of the evil in the world. Although Browning looked evil full in the face, wrote Osgood,

> . . . so balanced and normal was his mental and physical health, so all-embracing his love of things and human beings, that he could speak with certainty and authority based deeper than reason itself, "the communication," as he said, "of something more subtle than a ratiocinative process, when the convictions of 'genius' have thrilled my soul to its depths."[6]

Osgood, then, saw Browning's optimism based upon "certainty and authority . . . deeper than reason itself," a product of balance and insight, "mental and physical health," and "genius." On the other hand, Osgood would not have the timid reader frightened: "Far from being really subtle or esoteric it is obvious, and . . . as old as Plato. Love . . . is the supreme experience whereby we win intimations of what is perfect and infinite and immortal."[7]

Osgood, then, would have it both ways: in one case, Browning's philosophy is really simpler than it has been thought to be. In the other case, Browning's optimism has been oversimplified, until critics have lost sight of Browning's awareness of evil.

Other writers who in the Thirties gave Browning's thought favorable notice were Louis Cazamian, in *A History of*

[5]*Ibid.*
[6]*The Voice of England: A History of English Literature* (New York, 1952), p. 504.
[7]*Ibid.*

English Literature (1935), and Margaret Sherwood, in her book, *Undercurrents of Influence in English Romantic Poetry* (1934). The former, in his chapter on Browning, explained that the poet's "art is entirely pervaded by intellectual curiosity, and almost merged in the systematic quest of truth . . ."[8] At the base of the poet's philosophy, Cazamian, like Osgood, found his doctrine of love.[9] However, continued the French writer,

> Before such problems as that of immortality, Browning evinces the desire to believe, rather than actual faith. But his thinking is essentially positive, and Christian without being orthodox. And so he has become the recognized guide, the master of all who seek rationality and at the same time a creed; not only is he the prophet of a liberal religion, but his poetry has been an instrument of grace.[10]

This scholar's view of Browning's position as a teacher and religious leader is an interesting one, and there is a great deal of truth in what Cazamian wrote. He intimated that Browning, giving full assent to no creed, makes a broad appeal to readers of many religious shades. Secondly, he noted that Browning's positive rationalizing is attractive to those who like to think as well as believe. Thirdly, he stated that at least some of those who have accepted Browning as a prophet have benefited by doing so.

Margaret Sherwood's approach to the problem of bolstering Browning's reputation as a thinker is dual. On the one hand, she took pains to attack the adverse critics, Santayana in particular; on the other, she promulgated Browning's thought on its own merits. Browning, she held, had been

[8]Louis Cazamian, "Robert Browning," *A History of English Literature,* ed. Emile Legouis and Louis Cazamian (New York, 1935), p. 1229.
[9]*Ibid.,* p. 1232.
[10]*Ibid.*

"wiser in his generation than Mr. Santayana was in his."[11] According to her,

> ... Browning as a thinker was no barbarian; there was nothing primitive about his mental processes. He was an outstanding thinker of a wise, sophisticated, modern age, bringing piercing individual insight to bear upon the deeper thought of an epoch eager, original, swiftly advancing in knowledge, a great creative period. Browning's ethical idealism, based on thought, upon study of his fellows, upon experience, gives us an interpretation of life that is not to be ignored.[12]

"They are wrong," she continued, "who say that his work represents mere emotion; ... Intellect and feeling met and worked in happy fusion in his idealism...."[13] As I have pointed out above, however, the author of *Undercurrents* was not concerned solely with the negative side of Browning's reputation as a thinker. In addition to praising the poet as an original expressor of "the profoundest intuition of a great period,"[14] as one who found inspiration in a doctrine of universal love,[15] she climaxed her exaltation of Browning as a philosopher thus:

> ... the far-reaching thought of past ages, including that of the deep diviner of the ancient world,[16] and the profoundest utterances of Christian gospels are, in his thought, fused, and brought face to face with modern knowledge regarding the universe, and modern method of approach.[17]

Other authors who during the Thirties found elements of

[11]Margaret Sherwood, *Undercurrents of Influence in English Romantic Poetry* (Cambridge, Mass., 1934), p. 326.
[12]*Ibid.,* p. 323.
[13]*Ibid.,* p. 327.
[14]*Ibid.,* p. 266.
[15]*Ibid.,* pp. 334 ff.
[16]Plato?
[17]Sherwood, p. 349.

Browning's thought praiseworthy were not so wholehearted in their approval as Miss Sherwood and Professor Armstrong had been. Some gave partial approval to Browning's conclusions, while others touched only upon points of his philosophy which supported, illustrated, or were related to the subjects with which they were dealing.

Browning's optimism is a case in point. It has been shown above that Browning's more ardent supporters had been concerned with clearing the poet of the charge of flimsy, blind optimism. Likewise, other critics during the early Thirties— William Lyon Phelps, Stockton Axson, and Louise Zwager are examples—gave him at least indirect praise for his optimism, despite the fact that they did not give complete assent to his teachings. In 1932 Phelps called him "The greatest optimist of modern times,"[18] and both Axson and Louise Zwager defended his optimism. The last insisted that Browning did not preach that all really was right with the world, but that he really meant that everything in the world works toward good.[19] Axson describes as a "superficial view" that picture of Browning's optimism which describes it as easy-going.[20]

Another statement by William Lyon Phelps is an interesting commentary on Browning's reputation, for it displays both sides of a changed attitude. "When I was an undergraduate," he recalled, "nothing disgusted me more than to hear Browning's poetry praised as poetry. In my stupidity and ignorance, I insisted that he might be a profound philosopher, but that to rank him with Tennyson as a poet was blasphemy."[21] The implication of his statement seems to be that Browning had been underrated as a poet and perhaps overrated as a phi-

[18]*Robert Browning*, 2nd ed. (Indianapolis, 1932), p. 412.

[19]Louise H. Zwager, "Browning and Meredith as Poets of Man," *The English Philosophic Lyric* (Purmerend, 1931), p. 173.

[20]"Browning's Philosophy of Life," *Rice Institute Pamphlet*, XVIII (1931), 186.

[21]Phelps, *Robert Browning*, p. 429.

losopher. This conclusion is borne out by the fact that, in other chapters of *Robert Browning,* Phelps does not place particularly strong emphasis upon the validity of Browning's thought.

Two writers of the early Thirties awarded Browning at best qualified praise, relating his thought to the scientific advancements of his day. Ralph B. Crum found that Browning had been comparatively unaffected by the new sciences because he believed that love superseded any scientific truths. Since love, Browning reasoned, is primarily emotional and intuitional and since science is entirely intellectual, scientific knowledge is inferior to that which springs from the heart.[22] This dependence upon love, explained Crum, colored the poet's whole philosophy:

> Indeed, for him the Infinite Himself is a being who feels. Therefore, if the intellect attempted to negative this emotional truth, so much the worse for the intellect. Naturally this led to a certain distrust of knowledge in and for itself and tended to bring a dualism between feeling and intelligence which became the corner stone of his philosophy.[23]

That this dualism made it difficult for Browning to appraise adequately any conclusions of science is indicated by Crum when he wrote that "... before a scientific concept could assume any special significance for him, it must in turn be translated into terms of the emotions."[24]

Lionel Stevenson's primary concern with Browning in his *Darwin Among the Poets* (1932) was to show how the poet's thought seemed to reflect evolution. On the one hand, he held that Browning had been in partial agreement with evolutionary theory insofar as he found "in human imperfection

[22]Ralph B. Crum, *Scientific Thought in Poetry* (New York, 1931), pp. 192 ff.
[23]*Ibid.,* pp. 192–193.
[24]*Ibid.,* p. 194.

a promise of development still to come."[25] On the other hand, Stevenson seemed disappointed that Browning's thought did not show an increasing influence of evolutionary theory. Of *La Saisiaz,* a comparatively late poem, Stevenson wrote:

> Browning's universe is still the old anthropomorphic one.... His theory of development is exclusively a spiritual matter, more remote from the idea of physical evolution than it was when he wrote *Paracelsus* forty years before.[26]

Browning's failure to grasp scientific truth, as Crum noted, or to assimilate it, as Stevenson implied, is given further testimony in Joseph Warren Beach's *The Concept of Nature in Nineteenth-Century English Poetry,* published in 1936. The reader of Browning must always recall, warned Beach, "how completely his thinking was dominated by teleology— how little he thought in terms of causes and means, how much in terms of ends or 'final causes.' "[27] Further, Beach complained that Browning, seeing the soul from the point of view of orthodoxy, failed to conceive of a naturalistic soul.[28] In another place he argued that "Whatever reconciliation with nature appears in Browning is based upon the assumption that it includes for men a continued personal existence after death."[29]

However, the objections of Beach and Stevenson were, after all, comparatively minor. Browning's indifference to certain aspects of evolutionary thought and his ignorance of the supposed existence of a naturalistic soul were probably shared by many another writer and certainly are not particularly

[25]Lionel Stevenson, *Darwin Among the Poets* (Chicago, 1932), p. 45.

[26]*Ibid.,* p. 175.

[27]*The Concept of Nature in Nineteenth-Century English Poetry* (New York, 1936), p. 440.

[28]*Ibid.,* pp. 453–454.

[29]*Ibid.,* p. 445.

black spots upon his already tarnished reputation as a thinker in the Thirties.

The comparative dearth of praise of Browning's thought during the years 1930–1939 was quite naturally accompanied by a relative wealth of derogatory material, and the adverse criticism of the late Twenties continued in an uninterrupted flow through the Thirties. Let us begin with an estimate of Browning by F. L. Lucas in his *Eight Victorian Poets* (1930).[30]

It had long been the honored custom of the writers of literary histories to develop their criticisms of Browning by comparison and contrast with Tennyson. Likewise, the conclusion was most frequently drawn that Tennyson was the better artist and Browning the deeper thinker. In our own time the pendulum has swung in quite the other direction, but in 1930, Lucas was willing to dismiss both of the great Victorians as serious thinkers:

> Both he [Browning] and Tennyson seem to me pure poets damaged by being too much honoured as prophets in their own country. In consequence, they were led more and more to preach, where they should have sung. The mantle of Elijah was thrown upon them: under it they lost their vision and their heads.[31]

Further, calling Browning "a rather childish philosopher,"[32] he wrote "And so it is, I think, the Browning who feels, that matters. For his speculations were rather a South Sea Bubble, however brightly coloured."[33] To these deprecatory but general remarks on Browning's thought Lucas added an explanation of the uneven quality and the obscurity of much of Browning's verse:

[30]Quotations are taken from *Ten Victorian Poets* (Cambridge, 1940), the enlarged edition.
[31]*Ibid.*, p. 24.
[32]*Ibid.*, p. 25.
[33]*Ibid.*, p. 27.

It was partly sheer slovenliness; a man who could write a poem of fifty pages in double columns within seven weeks, and then print it from the first draft, leaving the punctuation to be corrected by a French friend, had the conscience of a pavement artist. Secondly, Browning had also a natural impediment of thought which made it hard for him to construct even an intelligible telegram.[34]

Since this impediment is one of thought rather than one of expression of thought, the charge made by Lucas is quite serious. The first charge is nearly as much so, in that it implies carelessness, a vice of no mean import to the reputation of the thinker. In fine, Lucas adjudged Browning a mixture of poet and poseur, one who under his difficult and careless prosody disguised himself as a philosopher:

It is indeed as if the curse of Browning's Paracelsus, a similar mixture of true poet and charlatan, had fallen on Browning himself:

"I cannot feed on beauty for the sake
Of beauty only, nor can drink in balm
From lovely objects for their loveliness . . .
I still must hoard and heap and class all truths
With one ulterior purpose: I must know!"

No doubt it succeeded for a time. It enabled persons who liked puzzles to suppose they liked poetry, and persons afraid of real thinking, to fancy themselves intellectual. And the thicker the incense rose from the Browning Societies, the more ragged and rugged his style became. It paid Browning then: since then it is Browning who pays.[35]

The comments of Lascelles Abercrombie, published in 1932, were not calculated to modify this view of Browning's think-

[34]*Ibid.*, p. 33.
[35]*Ibid.*, p. 35.

ing, although Abercrombie seemed to be attempting a two-sided picture. On the one hand, he made clear his belief that Browning was not wholly optimistic and that the poet's reputation had been ill-founded on that supposed virtue.[36] There was not, however, much else that Abercrombie would say in defense of Browning. That much of Browning's poetry deals with serious thought cannot be denied, he wrote, but this thought is

> ... not so much the *result* of thinking, in wise reflection and considerate judgment, as the very activity of thinking, the actual movement of ratiocination, and even casuistry. But this thought does not belong to the poet's matter: it belongs to his art. Browning is not thinking on his own account: he is attributing thought to certain characters he has imagined ...[37]

On the contrary, according to Abercrombie, when Browning is "thinking on his own account, and thinking, as his contemporary admirers awfully noticed, about the great problems of existence ... the matter of his poetry is of scarcely any importance at all."[38] As illustrations of his contention, the critic offered *La Saisiaz* and *Christmas-Eve and Easter-Day*. The thought presented in *La Saisiaz* he dismisses as "jejune and unexciting."[39] Of *Christmas-Eve*, he complained that

> ... the thought is a doggerel rendering of abysmally dull sectarian philosophy, futile, small, and profitless, which can never, one would think, have had much importance, and now

[36]Lascelles Abercrombie, "Robert Browning, 1812–1889," *The Great Victorians*, eds. H. J. and Hugh Massingham (New York, 1932), pp. 76–77.

[37]*Ibid.*, pp. 81–82.

[38]*Ibid.*, p. 82.

[39]*Ibid.*

has none whatever. Is this, we ask in our astonishment, this insignificant stuff, what a great poet calls thinking?[40]

Abercrombie's final objection to Browning's philosophical thought was directed at the poet's position in relation to the intellectual currents of his day. Accusing the poet of living in an "intellectual backwater," he wrote that "This would not have mattered if he had had any notable thought of his own. But he had not. . . ."[41] A necessary corollary is drawn: "He was like a war correspondent at the base, occasionally seeing, but never smelling, the smoke of powder, and cheerfully sending home encouraging messages, not very well informed, and of a most transitory importance."[42]

The points of Browning's philosophy which come under the heaviest fire in F. R. G. Duckworth's *Browning, Background and Conflict* (1932) include his doctrine of the infinite moment and his statements concerning eternal life. In these teachings about the nature of immortality and eternity Duckworth saw a deeply marked contradiction.[43] In certain places in Browning's poetry he found the promise of the "reward delayed, of the prize more valued and more valuable because it is out of the hand's grasp."[44] In other places he discovered Browning positing the soul "in a series of existences beyond the grave." To support this latter finding Duckworth quotes from *Old Pictures in Florence*:

> When the strong and the weak,
>   this world's congeries,
> Repeat in large what they
>   practised in small,

[40]*Ibid.*, p. 83.
[41]*Ibid.*
[42]*Ibid.*
[43]F. R. G. Duckworth, *Browning, Background and Conflict* (New York, 1932), p. 162.
[44]*Ibid.*, p. 151.

Through life after life in
unlimited series;
Only the scale's to be changed,
that's all.

and from *One Word More:*

Other heights in other lives,
God willing.

In still other poems, Duckworth found references to the realized, perfect moment as Browning's highest concept of eternity. This moment—coming as the true high point of an individual's life—this perfect moment, the writer insisted, is not compatible with the concept of endless striving. "This moment of crisis—this moment made eternity—cannot go on repeating itself endlessly in one existence after another. If it did, it would cease to be critical."[45] Summarizing this contradiction between endless striving and the eternal moment of bliss, the critic wrote: "To put it vulgarly, you cannot have it both ways."[46] That this contradiction is not a minor matter, one to be forgiven easily, was emphasized. Realizing that "we cannot demand from any poet, not even a philosophical poet like Browning, complete consistence or a rigidly determined system of beliefs," Duckworth wrote,

> yet in the points which have come under review here there is manifestly an incongruity which goes far and beyond what we are accustomed to find in the least philosophical of poets, a root contradiction as surprising and as significant as if we were to find embedded in the middle of Hardy's work, translated into the words and rhythms of Hardy, *Prospice* or the *Epilogue to Asolando.*[47]

[45]*Ibid.,* p. 181.
[46]*Ibid.,* p. 151.
[47]*Ibid.,* p. 182.

The difficulties involved in interpreting Browning's ideas about life after death were further illustrated by C. R. Tracy and H. V. Routh. Seeing Browning torn between the conservatism of his Nonconformist upbringing and the radicalism of his South Place associations, Tracy believed that *Easter-Day* intimates that Hell is merely the cessation of the growth of the spirit, but that *The Ring and the Book* implies that it is a place "where God unmakes but to remake the soul."[48] Routh, on the other hand, saw Browning a believer in another existence on earth, taking his cue from the line "No work begun shall ever pause for death." (*The Ring and the Book*, VII, 1787.) In Routh's words, "The spirit which could invigorate old age, could pass into another body and continue its progress towards self-fulfillment."[49]

As earlier chapters have shown, Browning's contradictory statements about the afterlife had been attacked steadily through the years. That this weakness has continued to be exploited by Browning's critics will be shown in the following chapters.

The adverse critics during the Thirties, however, had the field pretty much to themselves, and they did not hesitate to attack Browning's philosophy from more angles and at more points than those already mentioned. The tones of these criticisms, too, cover a wide range of attitudes, from the mildest regret to the sharpest scorn and sarcasm. An example of the former manner is that of J.M.D. Scott who, in explicating Browning's philosophy, noted almost sorrowfully that Browning could not fully appreciate the value of authority in life:

...though Browning inspires and encourages, he is not an

[48]"Browning's Heresies," *SP*, XXXIII (1936), 624–625. One can almost hear Omar-FitzGerald's cynical pot sneer, "What! did the hand, then, of the Potter shake?"

[49]*Towards the Twentieth Century: Essays in the Spiritual History of the Nineteenth* (New York, 1937), p. 103.

infallible guide in all problems of life. Courage and love will
carry us far, it is true, but the mind of man needs something
more, it demands security.... It seems, then, as if Browning
could only appreciate the principle of Divine guidance through
some mystical experience; as an Authority by which a man
shapes his earthly life it meant nothing to him.[50]

The stricture here is gentle enough, but of the other variety
we shall have sufficient samples.

Two writers of the middle Thirties, Betty MacCarthy and
Douglas Bush, indicated that Browning's reputation as a
thinker was held in generally low esteem. In *The Psychology
of Genius: Studies in Browning* (1936) the former noted
that the age had dealt unkindly with the great Victorians.
"Browning," she wrote, "with many of the literary heroes
of the last century, has fallen on evil days."[51] The latter
referred simply to "Browning's once exalted philosophy."[52]
An examination of the criticism of the middle and late
Thirties shows that the two last-mentioned writers had an-
alyzed the situation with more than a fair degree of accuracy.
In addition, both writers made further statements damaging
to the poet's reputation for serious thought. Betty Mac-
Carthy's remark, since it is concerned primarily with the
almost universally scoffed-at *Sordello,* is comparatively harm-
less: "In his efforts at condensing thought," she complained,
"he frequently skips necessary links in a sequence of ideas.
He throws us an inadequate key word to his mood, and leaves
us to struggle vainly in the meshes of his ambiguous expres-
sions."[53] Bush, on the other hand, implied another vain
struggle when he spoke of the poet as one who "lustily buffet-

[50]Quoted in Broughton, Northup, and Pearsall, p. 298.
[51]Betty G. MacCarthy, *The Psychology of Genius: Studies in
Browning* (London, 1936), p. vii.
[52]Douglas Bush, *Mythology and the Romantic Tradition in English
Poetry* (Cambridge, Mass., 1937), p. 358.
[53]MacCarthy, p. 76.

ing the waves of flux, solves all problems by shouting 'God! Life! Love!' "[54]

Other writers during the later years of the period 1930–1939 dealt more or less harshly with Browning's philosophy as it touched upon his religious credo. At least one writer, Philo Buck, found the poet "without real conviction."[55] Comparing Browning with Tennyson (whom he found "grasping at a straw in a sea of doubt"), Buck wrote that "Browning, though more vocal in his creed, and much more given to say 'I know,' than 'I believe,' has not much more genuine conviction to offer, when set beside a convinced poet, let us say Dante."[56]

But why, C. R. Tracy might have written, why attempt to prove that Browning is not a convinced poet like Dante when it is evident that he is incapable of intellectual conviction? Tracy, while writing his demonstration that Browning's religion is a sort of idealism, gave stern warning that "it is dangerous to apply the technical language of philosophy to so unsystematic and so unlearned a thinker as Browning . . ."[57] Calling the poet an "imperfect idealist because he never distinguished an idea from an emotion,"[58] Tracy went on to explain Browning's philosophy:

> His idealism, then, is an off-shoot of his theory of love decked out in philosophical jargon, and I doubt whether he had more than a superficial knowledge of the word as it is used by the Hegelian rationalists of his time.[59]

[54]Bush, p. 385.

[55]*The World's Great Age: The Story of a Century's Search for a Philosophy of Life* (New York, 1936), p. 308.

[56]*Ibid.*, p. 309.

[57]Tracy, pp. 619–620.

[58]*Ibid.*, p. 620.

[59]*Ibid.* Cf. Abercrombie's complaint that Browning stayed out of the current of contemporary thought, remained in an intellectual backwater.

H. B. Charlton, writing in 1938, accused Browning's readers of having misinterpreted the poet and of having made him what he was not. He wrote that "not a little encouraged by the latter Browning, readers are deluded into the view that Browning is primarily a thinker."[60] And, since some of the poet's supporters had presented *Rabbi Ben Ezra* and *An Epistle of Karshish* to readers as profoundly philosophical, Charlton retaliated:

> *Rabbi Ben Ezra* works within its intellectual assumptions and never questions them. *Karshish* is not concerned with philosophic grounds for belief in a God of love: it is entirely occupied with the depiction of the impact on a man's mind and feelings of the notion that there may be a God who is a God of love.[61]

Finally, as though in explanation of the current unpopularity of Browning's philosophy, he wrote that ". . . optimism hardly fits easily into the post-War world. Maybe the grounds of his faith were physiological rather than intellectual. Maybe, on the intellectual side, they presupposed an uncritically adopted theology."[62]

Whatever the explanations—and they are undoubtedly many and complex enough—the fact remains that the Thirties were, on the whole, exceedingly cold to Browning's philosophy. Where the period 1920–1929 could show at least four or five years during which Browning's thought was given a modicum of support and praise, the succeeding decade presented almost a solid front of hostility.

[60]H. B. Charlton, "Browning: The Poet's Aim," *Bulletin of the John Rylands Library,* XXII (1938), 99.

[61]*Ibid.,* p. 100.

[62]*Ibid.,* p. 103.

Stop playing, poet! May a brother speak? 'Tis you speak, that's your error. ✿ FROM TRANSCENDENTALISM

CONTINUED

THE YEARS 1940–1949 SAW PUBLISHED so little praise of Browning as a serious thinker that one is inclined to conclude that the supporters of Browning had given the cause up for lost. The tone of the unfavorable critics and the moderates as well indicates that they felt the battle to be over. The adverse critics showed (and were shown) far less hostility than their counterparts displayed two decades earlier, and, significantly, far fewer articles and books in this period treated Browning's philosophy of life. The changed approach to Browning is pointed up in striking fashion by a leading sentence in Hoxie N. Fairchild's "Browning's Heaven" : "Despite an ominous title, this essay will not revive the Victorian conception of Browning as a profound spiritual seer."[1] In the first place, the conception to which Fairchild alluded did live, as the earlier chapters of this study show, well beyond the Victorian era; but far more significant is the fact that the author of "Browning's Heaven" found it advisable to assure his readers that he was not a Browningite in the old sense of the word. Twenty years earlier, no such title would have been referred to as "ominous," even had it appeared in a more mundane publication than the *Review of Religion.*

One of the very few authors who published an endorsement of Browning's serious thought during the 1940's was Edwin Mims, who devoted a chapter of his *Great Writers as*

[1]Hoxie N. Fairchild, "Browning's Heaven," *Review of Religion,* XIV (1949), 30.

116

Interpreters of Religion (1945) to "Browning, Many-sided Poet of the Incarnation." Mims's statements were, however, so general that they did very little to shore up the walls against the rising tide of adverse criticism. He claimed all good things for Browning, whose "great voice . . . rings out, clear and strong," from the nineteenth century.[2] The poet "had a marvelous intellect"[3] and was "the friend and aid of those who would live in the spirit."[4] In addition, wrote Mims, Browning was fully acquainted with the thought of the ages, for *The Ring and the Book* demonstrates his appreciation of "the faith of the Middle Ages," and *Christmas-Eve* and *A Death in the Desert* prove him aware of contemporary thought.[5]

Briefer statements in praise of Browning were made by two other authors, Lord Dunsany and William O. Raymond. The former's remarks impress one as shallow, perhaps because he was concerned first of all with proving that Browning speaks for himself in *Bishop Blougram's Apology*. In the course of his argument, Dunsany wrote that Browning was a deeper thinker than either Tennyson or Arnold and that he was actually untouched by doubt.[6] Because of the generally high quality of Professor Raymond's work on Browning, one listens with greater interest to his praise. Raymond called the soliloquy of the Pope in *The Ring and the Book* "a definite summing up of Browning's philosophy of life, and a high watermark of metaphysical thought in nineteenth-

---

[2]*Great Writers as Interpreters of Religion* (Nashville, 1945), p. 168.
[3]*Ibid.*, p. 170.
[4]*Ibid.*, p. 169.
[5]*Ibid.*, pp. 170–172.
[6]"Browning Is Blougram," *The Nineteenth Century and After*, CXXXIX (1946), 177. William O. Raymond in another article suggests a somewhat different approach to the relationship of Browning to Blougram when he writes that "Browning is as deeply involved in this sophistry as his Roman Catholic Prelate." "Browning's Casuists," *SP*, XXXVII (1940), 659.

century poetry, enriched by acute religious perception."[7] But as one swallow does not make a summer, neither does one point of praise indicate any wholehearted agreement with or praise of Browning's philosophy of life, and Raymond pressed this point no further.

Although there was certainly no widespread approval of Browning's philosophy during the Forties, there was no real lack of interest in it. One side of this interest is displayed by the writers who continued to comment on different aspects of Browning's thought, sometimes explaining it, sometimes discussing its relationship to the serious thought of others, and sometimes merely recognizing its existence. These commentators served various purposes, not the least that of reminding the reading public of Browning's concern with matters of the intellect and of his once-exalted position as a thinker. Since these various moderate critics touched, in general, upon only a few points of Browning's thought—the value and uses of love, the nature of the afterlife of man's immortal soul, the proper sphere of action of the intellect, and the paradox of evil in a God-created world—it has seemed best to me to organize these topically, so that the middle-of-the-road criticism on any one subject can be seen at a glance.

On the whole, the moderate writers during the Forties seem to have been sympathetic towards, if not in agreement with, Browning's conception of the nature of evil in the world and of its place in the struggle of the human soul for perfection. Most of these writers either indicated or attempted to explain Browning's belief that evil is only apparent or at worst only temporary. Writing in 1943, one author, Troy Organ, distinguished between various classes of evil and attempted to show how Browning would have dealt with each.[8] Although the writer's method of distinctions

[7]"Browning's Poetry Fifty Years After," *University of Toronto Quarterly*, IX (1940), 139.

[8]"Browning's Message for Dark Days," *College English*, V, 13–18.

would scarcely pass muster with the writers of philosophy textbooks, it served his purpose and deserves recounting here. Organ found evil classifiable into the following categories: natural evil (earthquakes, floods, etc.), circumstantial evil (accidents, "fate"), physical evil (pain), intellectual evil (doubts, uncertainties), evils of disposition (greed, anger, hate), moral evils (sins), and the evil of perfection. None of these, wrote Organ, with the possible exception of the last, would the poet have considered really evil. The first three constitute mere obstacles in man's way, obstacles to be overcome. As for the existence of doubts and uncertainties, Browning would have found them not undesirable but even necessary for the development of the soul. Likewise, the moral evils serve to produce the conflicts one must endure in order to become strong. Concerning evils of disposition, the author of "Browning's Message for Dark Days" found only that Browning would have insisted that all acts, evil ones as well as good, be performed wholeheartedly. And finally, there is no evil at all, unless it be perfection, that notorious "gravestone of growth."

This last, however, would seem to be a conclusion to be accepted guardedly. For if perfection be evil in Browning's philosophy, and if Heaven contain the perfect circles that on earth are the broken arcs, then Browning is forced immediately to the conclusion of the syllogism. These conflicts presented by the existence of evil in the world were recognized by Organ, and he concluded only that Browning's own conclusions are inconsistent, adding, "as all such solutions must be."[9]

The moderate critics were interested also in another side of the picture of evil in the world: If evil is only apparent, what becomes of man's moral responsibility? If there is no evil, man can do no evil. The advantage of this condition to

[9]*Ibid.*, p. 18.

the Pilgrim on the way to the Heavenly City is obvious: he can tarry as long as he likes at Vanity Fair. To change the figure, the seaman who accepts this position without qualification can, if he wishes, simply lift his oars into the boat, feeling secure that God will pull him in to shore despite his failure to row. In short, there is no moral responsibility whatever if there is no evil to choose or reject. In 1940 J. M. Ariail alluded to the fact that Browning evidently did not believe in the final reality of evil, for he remarked that the poet simply refused—in *Apparent Failure*, for example—"to give a man up for lost."[10] On the other hand, H. B. Charlton seemed to reject such a conclusion, writing that in Browning's poetry there is moral growth only where there is stress, strain on the soul,

> ... an exercise of free choice where there is knowledge of good and evil. Remove freedom, remove evil, and morality has been destroyed. Wherefore life is an invigorating adventure in personal responsibility and that is the one way in which a man can at one and the same time save his soul and the soul of humanity.[11]

Perhaps the explanation of Browning's position on the existence of evil was stated with more exactness by Samuel C. Chew in his chapter on Browning in *A Literary History of England*.[12] Remarking upon Browning's preoccupation with the seeming contradiction of evil in God's world, he wrote that for the poet

> Evil and falsehood have no real existence in themselves but

[10]"Is 'Pippa Passes' a Dramatic Failure?" *SP*, XXXVII (1940), 125.

[11]"Browning's Ethical Poetry," *Bulletin of the John Rylands Library*, XXVII (1942), 69.

[12]"The Brownings," *The Nineteenth Century and After* (Albert C. Baugh *et al.*, *A Literary History of England* [New York, 1948], Vol. IV), pp. 1393–1404.

are manifestations by contrariety of love and truth. Care and pain are pledges of the divine regard. Strength comes from an obstructed road; assurance would breed torpor, but difficulty increases power. The thought is in line with German idealism which taught that the imagination creates evil in order that by combatting it the moral will may be strengthened. Hence "the paradox that comforts while it mocks," the doctrine of the spiritual value of failure. This doctrine, which the poet's contemporaries found of inestimable worth, our generation has contemptuously rejected, perhaps because our failures have been incalculably disastrous and our values have gone awry.[13]

The contradictory nature of Browning's varying concepts of an afterlife did not fail to draw forth expositions from the moderate critics during the Forties, although these appeared by no means as frequently as they had in decades past. The picture presented by Browning in the close of Guido Francheschini's final monologue, in *The Last Ride Together,* and in *Old Pictures in Florence,* in *Rabbi Ben Ezra,* and in *La Saisiaz* is by no means an harmonious one, and the obvious inconsistencies in Browning's views of eternity find their confusions mirrored in the statements of the critics who attempted to explain without condemning the poet's conclusions. J. M. Ariail's account of Browning on the subject of afterlife is typical. He wrote of Browning:

He shows little interest in heaven as it is usually thought of, less interest in hell, but great interest in eternity. Salvation, for him, meant, frequently, the learning of one truth, eyes opened to the eternal verities, the recognition of the superiority of good over evil, of love over hate, of truth over error, of purity over a stain. It meant the recognition of one's failures: it sometimes meant an attitude.[14]

[13]*Ibid.,* p. 1400.
[14]Ariail, p. 122.

This same confusion is not to be found in the interpretations given *La Saisiaz* during this decade. Several authors seemed to be in agreement on this poem of Browning's. Herbert J. C. Grierson and J. C. Smith concluded that in *La Saisiaz* Browning "argues that immortality is, and ought to be, a matter of faith, not of knowledge."[15] The same attitude is reflected in H. B. Charlton's comment that in this poem Browning "was led to complete agnosticism, though not, of course to religious unbelief."[16] Samuel C. Chew likewise noted in this poem an "uncharacteristic gloom," a proof that Browning "did not easily come by his assurance of God's love."[17] Hoxie N. Fairchild saw an attempt by Browning to argue for immortality without explicit reference to Christianity[18] and an example of Browning's movement toward "a vague subjective theism in which Christian belief counted for little or nothing."[19] It will be seen later that Fairchild's general view of the poet's varying statements about eternity is not a favorable one.

Nearly everyone in every decade considered here agreed that Browning put an extremely high value on love, although the critics did not always exonerate him from the charge of overstressing its value. Among those critics who neither praised greatly nor disparaged the position Browning gave to love, one might mention Samuel C. Chew, Troy Organ, H. B. Charlton, and William J. Tucker. Chew found that his doctrine of love gave the poet a basis for faith,[20] and Organ judged love Browning's ultimate reality.[21] Charlton, on the other hand,

[15]"Robert Browning," *A Critical History of English Poetry* (London, 1947), p. 420.
[16]"Browning's Ethical Poetry," p. 41.
[17]Chew, p. 1398.
[18]"La Saisiaz and the Nineteenth Century," *Modern Philology*, XLVIII (1948), 105.
[19]*Ibid.*, p. 105.
[20]Chew, p. 1399.
[21]Organ, p. 18.

questioned the relationship between lust and love in Browning's poetry and concluded that the poet, in *The Statue and the Bust,* at least, would have defended himself by saying, "The beginning of love may be mere brute appetites, but it is an appetite if brutish yet a truth."[22] Tucker's view of the importance of love in Browning's philosophy was somewhat differently expressed:

> Browning is pre-eminently a love mystic. Love is for him the underlying principle which explains the universe. The mystic side of human love is suggested tenderly and wistfully in such poems as "Evelyn Hope" and "Two in the Compagna." In both poems, love is an ideal as well as a reality, and being an ideal its complete satisfaction can never be attained— hence the divine discontent of the human heart.[23]

Although, as will be seen, some of the critics writing between 1940 and 1949 attacked Browning for his extreme distrust of man's intellect, there were a few writers who contented themselves with explaining or illustrating this distrust of human reason. Thus, Charlton found Browning an intellectual agnostic in *La Saisiaz,*[24] and felt that *Bishop Blougram's Apology* "both justifies and depicts this limitation of human reasoning powers."[25] Chew referred to this distrust of the intellect in connection with Browning's religious beliefs when he wrote that the poet "In general . . . was convinced of the superiority of the intuitive faculties over the intellectual in giving man a knowledge of God."[26] C. Willard Smith implied that Browning positively desired to degrade the intellectual faculty:

[22]"Browning's Ethical Poetry," p. 57.
[23]"The Mystic Note in English Verse," *The Catholic World,* CLXVII (1948), 422.
[24]"Browning's Ethical Poetry," p. 41.
[25]"Browning as Poet of Religion," *Bulletin of the John Rylands Library,* XXVII (1943), 299.
[26]Chew, p. 1400.

The formulation of systems of thought and the inclinations of the formulators of systems to diminish truth into fine points of demonstrable fact were, in his opinion, to be mistrusted, for to prove the point was to remove the mystery. For him the essential fact, in both poetry and religion, was the immediate presence of the mystery, the flowing river of light of his poetic and religious vision.[27]

In the earlier decades of this century there were innumerable brief comments and passing remarks to indicate Browning's recognized position as a serious thinker, but such evidences of high repute were few in the Forties. These comments are miscellaneous in nature and only faded reflections of a once bright reputation for deep thought: "Browning is very much more of a mystic poet than Tennyson,"[28] and Browning chose "the poet's way to philosophical and theological truth" which "has a validity of its own, and is most valid where the poet is most poetic,"[29] or "every typical idea Browning ever expressed in his poetry may be found implicit or expressed in the first three poems."[30]

The adverse criticism of Browning's thought was both specific in nature and severe in tone during the 1940's. It differs somewhat from the earlier adverse criticisms in that it assumed an air of confidence and was not so much concerned with attacking the Browningites as the critics of earlier decades had been. There was an underlying assumption that the Browning balloon had already been pretty well deflated and that the purpose of further criticism was simply to add evidence to a case already won.

[27]*Browning's Star-Imagery: The Study of a Detail in Poetic Design* (Princeton, 1941), p. 242.

[28]Tucker, p. 421.

[29]Charlton, "Browning as Poet of Religion," p. 273.

[30]Stewart Walker Holmes, "Browning's *Sordello* and Jung: Browning's *Sordello* in the Light of Jung's Theory of Types," *PMLA,* LVI (1941), 796.

The tone of George Santayana's utterance in 1940 is an excellent example of this new note in Browning criticism. Forty years earlier he had been one of the very few who had condemned Browning's philosophy *in toto*, and, flying in the face of general critical opinion, he had been careful to document his attack and to point out qualities of Browning's poetry which he felt had led the poet's followers to regard him as a serious thinker. In other words, Santayana in 1900 was well aware that he was a breaker of new ground, and although his attack was most severe, it was also most careful. On the other hand, in his "A General Confession," published in 1940, the critic-philosopher accepted the destruction of Browning's reputation as a thinker as a *fait accompli*.[31] Lumping together Royce, Hegel, Nietzsche, and Browning, Santayana wrote:

That which repelled me in all these men was the survival of a sort of forced optimism and pulpit unction, by which a cruel and nasty world, painted by them in the most lurid colours, was nevertheless set up as the model and standard of what ought to be. The duty of an honest moralist would have been rather to distinguish, in this bad or mixed reality, the part, however small, that could be loved and chosen from the remainder, however large, which was to be rejected and denounced.[32]

The assumption is clear: his early indictment of Browning as a dishonest moralist has been borne out by the succeeding generations. Indeed, in the same volume, Philip Blair Rice commented on "The Poetry of Barbarism," saying that Browning's ". . . moral and theological ideas are of course easy game

[31]Santayana's steady disapproval of Browning's philosophy has been very briefly traced by R. H. Bowers in his "Santayana and Browning: A Postscript," *N&Q*, CXCIV (1949), 433–434.

[32]*The Philosophy of George Santayana*, ed. Paul Arthur Schlipp (Evanston and Chicago, 1940), p. 11.

for Santayana," and that the early article "supplied . . . a needed deflation of Browning."[33]

Nor did William O. Raymond and B. Ifor Evans, both writing in 1940, help to improve the impoverished condition of Browning's reputation as a thinker. Writing about "Browning's Casuists," the former found that "In an attempt to vindicate his ethical convictions and to establish a firm basis for his religious faith, Browning is driven to place all stress on love, and by contrast to debase reason."[34] Finally, Raymond remarked that when he deals with reason and man's intellectual faculties, the poet is "obviously entangled" in casuistry.[35] Evans' objections to Browning's thought seem to have been based upon a belief that Browning steered clear of the intellectual life of his own day: "If he was to be a philosopher in verse he would have done well to know his own age more fully. Italy, though he seems to people it with so many living people, was a retreat from a world he never faced."[36]

Other objections registered in the early Forties include Henri Peyre's criticism that in his later work Browning's "message had degenerated into shallow optimism, his tricks of psychology and versification had grown effete."[37] There is here the implication, however, that Browning's message was more vital in his earlier works. An apparent source of irritation to H. B. Charlton was the potter's wheel metaphor in *Rabbi Ben Ezra*, so often praised by Browning's supporters as a remarkable philosophical poem. This metaphor, wrote Charlton,

> . . . makes man entirely a creature without creative power in himself: and that is contrary to Browning's full awareness

[33]*Ibid.*, p. 286.
[34]Raymond, "Browning's Casuists," p. 642.
[35]*Ibid.*, p. 657.
[36]B. Ifor Evans, *Tradition and Romanticism* (New York, 1940), p. 170.
[37]*Writers and Their Critics: A Study of Misunderstanding* (Ithaca, 1944), p. 43.

of life's elements. So he gives to the clay an incongruous knowledge of its own purpose, and an equally incongruous capacity to participate in its own unending making.[38]

Charlton did not make clear whether Browning was fully aware of the "incongruities" spotted in the passage just quoted, but in any case he judged Browning guilty of an artistic, if not a logical, error.

An attack of far greater severity than the criticisms already noted was made by Stewart Walker Holmes in 1945.[39] This critic branded Browning a "semantic stutterer," explaining the term by saying:

> To be more precise, when the poet wrote as a prophet, as a metaphysician, he lost the ability to write meaningfully, chiefly because, like stutterers of the kitchen garden variety, he confused levels of abstractions and dealt with the thing-word relationship intensionally rather than extensionally.[40]

Holmes supported his contention that Browning was unable to express himself meaningfully about matters metaphysical in the complexities of *Sordello,* in the fact that Browning always avoided discussing "deep" subjects with others, and in his implying frequently that his so-called obscurity was a fault in his readers, not in his poetry.[41] Browning's semantic difficulties, Holmes averred, were due first of all to his faulty training in the use of language and, second, to his faulty processes of evaluation.

Browning's abilities as a thinker, then, are rated quite low by Holmes. It will be noted that his attack is even more severe than those made by critics like Lascelles Abercrombie—to take

[38]Charlton, "Browning's Ethical Poetry," p. 63.
[39]"Browning: Semantic Stutterer," *PMLA,* LX (1945), 231–255.
[40]*Ibid.,* p. 231.
[41]*Ibid.,* pp. 232 ff. Holmes cites a number of specific examples of what he considers confusions caused by Browning's semantic difficulties.

a convenient example from the preceding decade. For, although Abercrombie found Browning's thought in *Christmas-Eve* "insignificant," Holmes judged him incapable of even insignificant thought on metaphysical or theological subjects. This criticism marks a low point in the Forties and was, in a way, the most complete condemnation of Browning's thought before 1950.

Writers in the years nearing the close of the period 1940–1949 did not follow Holmes's lead in denying that Browning had the ability to communicate reasonably well, but nevertheless the criticisms by Donald Smalley and William Clyde DeVane were, in their own way, equally damning.[42] They dealt principally with Browning's inability to maintain an open mind.

In explaining Browning's mistaken portrait of Thomas Chatterton, Smalley wrote that "Such was the peculiar cast of Browning's creative thinking that he could twist fact itself to his artistic ends with a confident hand, assured that even in doing so he was serving the cause of historical truth."[43] This confidence, Smalley implied, was the result of "a curious process of self-hypnosis."[44] He further commented that "This Essay allows us to see more clearly than before that Browning was in manner and method neither a scientist nor an intuitive psychoanalyst."[45] One more remark by Smalley, a reference to the fact that Browning had a "remarkable habit of creative reading,"[46] has a distinct bearing on our subject in that if this comment has a basis in fact, then it must be concluded that Browning's mind functioned so illogically that he was unable not only to express himself meaningfully but also to read "meaningfully."

One is prompted at once to turn back to Dean DeVane's

[42]See Donald Smalley, *Browning's Essay on Chatterton*, Foreword by William Clyde DeVane (Cambridge, Mass., 1948).
[43]*Ibid.*, p. 53.
[44]*Ibid.*
[45]*Ibid.*, p. 77.
[46]*Ibid.*, p. 86.

foreword for assurance that Smalley's judgment is too astrin-
gent, but such assurance is not forthcoming. DeVane wrote:

> The truth is that Browning was incapable of reading history
> or penetrating the secret of historical characters. This is a
> harsh judgment, but a true one. The reason for it is very
> clear, however; it is that Browning was by temperament a hot
> partisan, and came to every cause with a mind already set
> in a pattern which made him pre-judge every case from in-
> tensely personal predilections. As Professor Smalley wisely
> says, Browning could only dissect what he had first created.[47]

Except for the reputation and acknowledged good judgment
of the author of that last statement, one might be led to shrug
it off as an example of an extreme position, merely another
blanket condemnation. But DeVane is no iconoclast, and the
effect of the statement is to disqualify not only Browning's
methods as an historian, as DeVane pointed out, but also
his methods as a thinker, for the man who approaches any
new concept, matter, or situation with "a mind already set
in a pattern" can scarcely deal with it either honestly or in
logical fashion. He may come to right conclusions, but he can
hardly come to them in the right ways.

Further, in an article published in 1947, DeVane commented
adversely on *Christmas-Eve and Easter-Day*, a work frequently
praised as a clear statement of Browning's religious position.
In particular, he spoke of Browning's discussion of faith and
doubt: "In spite of many splendid passages the result was not
significant for its day, and is even less so for ours."[48] In the
same vein are the remarks of H. J. C. Grierson and J. C.
Smith, published in the same year in their *A Critical History
of English Poetry*. These authors commented on "his poems of
religion, which comforted many tender souls in that Victorian

[47]*Ibid.,* p. vii.
[48]William Clyde DeVane, "The Virgin and the Dragon," *Yale
Review,* XXXVII (1947), 38.

twilight of faith, though his arguments, being the arguments of a poet, are sometimes no more than extended metaphors."[49] Their conclusions about the poet's stature as a thinker are also of interest. Grierson and Smith explained: "In his own day, Browning was over-rated as a thinker and underrated as a poet. His own philosophy . . . was not really new, though he applied it with amazing freshness to many novel situations."[50]

It is probably Browning's application of his thought "to many novel situations" that Samuel C. Chew alluded to when he wrote: "The number and variety of the men and women whom he created make for the illusion that Browning possessed a wide range of ideas; but the fact is that he illustrated by innumerable case-histories a small recurring group of themes."[51] Although Chew's chapter on Browning is not, on the whole, unfriendly to the poet, a number of statements such as this last indicate that the author of *The Nineteenth Century and After* was not at all in agreement with Browning's philosophy of life. Commenting on Browning's faith and optimism, Chew found the poet seeking "assurance in an illogical and paradoxical attainment of faith through doubt; St. Michael stands the more secure just because he feels the serpent writhe beneath his feet."[52] Chew was critical of Browning's grounds for belief in immortality, finding that Browning's argument based on the evils and imperfections of this life is not supported and that "No shadow of proof is offered" for the assertion that "Virtue and happiness will ultimately be brought into harmony with one another through the agency of God."[53] Finally, advancing one reason why "Much of his work is dead," Chew said that Browning "too often sank the poet in the teacher."[54]

[49]Grierson and Smith, p. 418.
[50]*Ibid.*, p. 420.
[51]Chew, p. 1402.
[52]*Ibid.*, p. 1400.
[53]*Ibid.*, p. 1401.
[54]*Ibid.*, p. 1402.

Perhaps the muddled and contradictory statements made since 1930 about Browning's concept of an afterlife deterred other writers in the Forties from touching the subject; perhaps the critics felt that the subject ought simply to be left closed or that it was too unimportant to resurrect. At any rate the adverse critics made few attempts to get at the heart of the matter. One treatment mentioned in the opening paragraphs of this chapter, Hoxie N. Fairchild's "Browning's Heaven," was published in 1949 and could have done no good to the poet's reputation as a serious thinker. Fairchild's final remarks on the inconsistent nature of Browning's conceptions of immortality summed up a line of thinking that cannot reconcile the contradictory elements in Browning's beliefs:

> He wished to think of heaven as a state in which the probationary struggle would be rewarded by the gift of "one good fair wise thing;" but he had committed himself so recklessly to mere energy worship that at last he was compelled to project life's muddle beyond the gates of death.... For me, however, the "Epilogue" to *Asolando* marks the outcome of a great spiritual tragedy. Others must "Greet the unseen with a cheer."[55]

In another article published in 1949, Fairchild touched upon another point, a slighter one to be sure, but one which added no laurels to Browning's reputation for serious thought. Calling the poet "the Simple-Hearted Casuist," he displayed a subtle approach to Browning's distrust of the reasoning faculties of man, showing that in many poems—*An Epistle of Karshish, Bishop Blougram's Apology, The Ring and the Book,* and *Mr. Sludge, the Medium* are examples—Browning steps personally into the argument in order to reveal clearly to the readers that devious villains are weaving tissues of lies and

[55]Fairchild, "Browning's Heaven," p. 37.

webs of deceit.[56] In short, Browning's distrust of reason made him fear that the intellects of his readers were incapable of separating the strands of truth from the welter of lies.

Indirectly, of course, the various writers who during the Forties found that Browning rejected reason and the intellect in solving his problems, metaphysical or otherwise, were registering one further objection against the proponents of Browning as a deep thinker. For if the systematic thinker refuses to recognize reason as the method by which he can form judgments and reach conclusions, he rules out of consideration one of his primary tools and is reduced to an absolute reliance on intuition.

In the period 1940–1949, then, Browning's reputation for serious thought fared no better than it had during the 1930's. His methods of thinking and the conclusions to which he came alike were attacked from many quarters. Most of the critics found Browning's position on such matters as love, immortality, evil, and the uses of reason and the intellect not to their liking. Further, although there is no absolute unanimity of opinion to be discerned during these years, Browning's partisans were considerably fewer in number than they once had been and were, as far as I can judge, less effective than his opponents. Despite the occasional praise of a writer like Mims, the general climate of opinion was very definitely unfavorable as it touched upon Browning's abilities to approach ideas in the proper frame of mind and to present arguments logically and effectively. On the whole, the critics during this period were pretty well agreed that Browning's mind fell below their standards for serious thinkers.

[56]Fairchild, "Browning the Simple-Hearted Casuist," *University of Toronto Quarterly,* XVIII (1949), 234–240.

Hence, on the whole, I conclude that this particular devil is not quite so black . . . ✿ BROWNING TO ISABELLA BLAGDEN

UP FROM NADIR

SINCE 1950 THERE HAS BEEN A MARKED increase of interest in the great Victorians, and Browning has not been neglected. If one can judge by the number of books and articles dealing with the poet—most of them sound, many of them scholarly, a few of them daring—he is not considered dead weight by our contemporaries. Newly edited letters, a most useful bibliography, a revised edition of the best of Browning handbooks, a psychological study, a "new critical" analysis—these publications, combined with other factors, have stimulated fresh work in every area. The effect of this rather intensive critical and scholarly interest upon Browning's reputation as a thinker, I hope to demonstrate in this chapter.

This is not to say that Browning's reputation as a thinker underwent a dramatic change for the better in 1950. On the contrary, the majority of the commentators since 1950 have done one of three things: they have attacked Browning's thought or those who promoted the concept of the poet as a teacher-philosopher; they have taken for granted that the concept is an already burst bubble; or, a deadly sign, they have simply ignored Browning the Philosopher and have concentrated on Browning the Poet. We shall do well to begin with those critics who have continued the now well-established and very nearly time-honored tradition of deprecating Browning's philosophy and "message."

Published in 1950, John Heath-Stubbs's *The Darkling Plain* will serve as an excellent point of departure. Like many another describer of the Victorian intellectual battleground,

133

Heath-Stubbs has found helpful the device of discussing Tennyson and Browning by means of comparison and contrast.
The virtues he attributes to these Victorian giants do not include valid and serious thought, for he finds their verses "intellectually unsatisfying" and writes that "Fundamentally,
these two most eminent of the Victorian poets are dishonest."[1]
The two of them do better, says Heath-Stubbs, when they are
unconcerned with "a duty to teach or to demonstrate a psychological—i.e., a scientific—truth."[2] The author of *The
Darkling Plain,* then, objects to going to the poets for a message or for truth and, presumably, finds their didacticism and
moralizing—or at least that which has been extolled as such—
worthless. In these statements are rejected the dicta of that
group of Victorian writers and appreciators who can justly
be said to have been instrumental in the formation of a
Browning cult.

Further, there are found in Heath-Stubbs's book specific
objections against Browning alone. There is reference, for
example, to "Browning's tortuous thickets of half-digested
thought"[3] and to an optimism "more emphatically than consistently or convincingly expressed."[4] Again, there is a reference to a belief that Browning did not recognize or grasp "the
social evils and disruption of his day,"[5] a reminiscence of the
old charge by Abercrombie that Browning lived in intellectual
backwaters. In view of the possible objection that at least
Browning was highly cognizant of and fully conversant with
the so-called Higher Criticism, Heath-Stubbs writes that such
poems as *A Death in the Desert* and *An Epistle of Karshish,*

... though they attempt a direct intellectual treatment of the

[1] John Heath-Stubbs, *The Darkling Plain* (London, 1950), pp.
98–99.
[2] *Ibid.,* p. 148.
[3] *Ibid.,* p. 59.
[4] *Ibid.,* p. xiii.
[5] *Ibid.,* p. 99.

question of the historical development of religion, have for all
of their brilliance something academic about them. They are
writings round and about the subject, where neither intuitive
faith nor honest doubt speaks clearly.[6]

Published in the *Yale Review* in 1952, Richard D. Altick's
"The Private Life of Robert Browning" is wholly condemna-
tory in tone. Although Altick leaves himself open to critical
attack by what seems to be an extremely wide application of
certain psychological approaches, there is neither room nor
reason to do more here than to discuss his approach as it
affects Browning's thought and his reputation for it. Altick's
attack is reminiscent of that made by Stewart Walker Holmes
six years earlier in that both seem to rate Browning's mental
abilities below those of the average person. Both, in fact, seem
surprised that Browning, endowed with such poor intellectual
capacities, was able even occasionally to produce understandable or effective poetry. Indeed, Altick writes in explanation of
this phenomenon that "Nature had lavished gifts and aspirations upon him, but they were so mixed and contradictory that
only by a fortunate miracle did some of them conjoin to produce the rich poetry by which he is remembered."[7] Although
this remark is too broad, one cannot easily dismiss the
objections Altick raises against Browning's thinking. If we
overlook for the time the critic's concern with proving that
robustness indicates unhealthiness or that a Freudian approach is necessary in understanding Browning, we can give
fairer treatment to his complaint against the poet's mental
ability. Two points registered against the poet are described
as "verbal inadequacy" and "lack of mental discipline."[8] The
former characteristic is explained in part as Browning's inability to know what he wanted his readers to understand

[6]*Ibid.,* p. 98.
[7]"The Private Life of Robert Browning," *Yale Review,* XLI (1952),
261–262.
[8]*Ibid.,* pp. 251–252.

from his poetry; somehow, according to Altick, Browning frequently failed to communicate. The second fault is attributed in part to Browning's "extraordinarily swift faculty of association," a faculty which he either could not or would not keep under control.

The next point treated here is, in a sense, better documented. Altick writes of Browning:

> ... actually he was not a thinker at all, either by native gift or by training. His reading in the classics of Western philosophy was unsystematic and spotty. Neo-Platonism he was well acquainted with—witness "Abt Vogler," one of the most Neo-Platonic poems of recent centuries—but he blandly admitted to Mrs. Orr that "he knew neither the German philosophers nor their reflection in Coleridge." What he read, he did not always understand; he ludicrously misinterpreted Mandeville's "Fable of the Bees." Compared with Tennyson or Arnold or Newman, he was philosophically illiterate, and he probably knew it. In social conversation he always shied away from serious subjects.[9]

This excerpt illustrates pretty well Altick's opinion of Browning's position among thinkers: he is far inferior to his contemporaries Tennyson, Arnold, and Newman, although the philosophies of none of these received the attention Browning's did.

Like Heath-Stubbs, Altick makes something of Browning's failure to grasp contemporary thought, especially the "historical" criticism of Christianity. Instead of answering the critics, writes Altick, Browning did no more than reaffirm his intuitive belief, repeating for the sake of convincing himself, "I believe ... I believe ... I believe ... of course I believe."[10] In line with this intuitive approach, Altick judges Browning's rejection of the claims of the intellect. "He was a

[9]*Ibid.*, p. 258.
[10]*Ibid.*, p. 259.

born dialectician," writes Altick, "yet he was bidden by his deeper self to deny the efficacy of all reason.... He was obliged to load the dice against every speaker in his poems who chose to vindicate himself by reason rather than by intuition."[11]

Perhaps the severity—certainly the effectiveness—of Altick's attack is blunted by his psychological approach. However, the article is of great importance to this study, for it marks a very low point of Browning's reputation as a thinker. The sum of the critic's attitude is simply this: Browning was incapable of serious thought on any matter of importance. It is not merely an attack against conclusions that Browning reached or any message he conveyed, but a complete denial that Browning could or did think effectively.

Nor is the portrait painted the same year by Geoffrey Tillotson in his *Criticism and the Nineteenth Century* one whit more flattering to Browning or, for that matter, to Tennyson, since both are included in a blanket stricture. Speaking of Browning's *Easter-Day* and Tennyson's *Two Voices*, both of which apparently represented the poets' grounds for the acceptance of faith, Tillotson writes:

> We know all too well what those flattering mornings turned into: the poets should have looked longer and seen that their dawns were false. Some poets kept on thinking with more consistency, or for longer without collapsing: Clough, Fitzgerald, Meredith and Hardy, for instance.[12] But even in the thoughtful poems of these stalwarts, there is still present that consoling ambiguity of poetry. Thinking, we feel, is not quite so binding when it has chosen for its medium verse instead of prose. Poetry, in the nineteenth century as always, was a

[11]*Ibid.,* p. 261.

[12]These instances, together with the quotation from Housman which concludes the paragraph, are evidence enough of Tillotson's own views on optimism.

refuge for thinkers. The poets think as long as they can, then they

> "fasten
> Their hands upon their hearts."[13]

Like Altick, then, Tillotson finds Browning a poorer thinker than certain of his contemporaries. He is accused of inconsistencies and, perhaps, of hiding behind the skirts of the muse, hands clutched fast against his heart.

Disparagement of Browning's intellect has come as well in the Fifties from the English branch of the New Critics, more specifically from F. R. Leavis in his 1950 edition of *New Bearings in English Poetry*. Riding his thesis that English poetry from the time of the Romantics was in desperate need of a new direction, Leavis brings Browning to the whipping post for a brief moment, long enough to add his scorn to the great weight which had been bearing down on the poet's reputation as a thinker. Writes Leavis:

> Browning would have been less robust if he had been more sensitive and intelligent. He did indeed bring his living interests into his poetry, but it is too plain that they are not the interests of an adult sensitive mind.[14]

The editor of the now-defunct *Scrutiny* continues in this vein, remarking tartly that "It is possible to consider him as a philosophical or psychological poet only by confusing intelligence with delight in the exercise of certain grosser cerebral muscles."[15] The closest Browning comes to receiving praise in Leavis' book is the author's admission that Ezra Pound (in

[13]*Criticism and the Nineteenth Century* (London, 1951), p. 215. Tillotson credits Housman, *Last Poems*, X ("Could man be drunk for ever . . .").
[14]*New Bearings in English Poetry* (London, 1950), p. 20.
[15]*Ibid.*

the select circle—with T. S. Eliot and Gerard Manley Hopkins—of three poets who led poetry in the desired new direction) had profited by a study of Browning. "But so inferior a mind and spirit as Browning's," continues Leavis quickly, "could not provide the impulse needed to bring back into poetry the adult intelligence."[16]

Less intentional, probably, and perhaps less significant, is the failure of certain other writers during the period 1950–1956 to add anything to the reputation Browning once had for valuable intellectual activity. In his article on a minor point in *The Ring and the Book*, William Coyle pokes his small hole in the fabric of Browning's scholarly understanding, already tattered by such expositions as Donald Smalley's *Browning's Essay on Chatterton*, when he writes that the poet "apparently confounded Molinos' teachings with Jansenism."[17] A minor point, but one that impugns one or more of the following: Browning's scholarship, his ability to understand, or his desire to treat facts carefully.

Browning's biographers, with the exception of Dallas Kenmare, whose work will be considered below, do not attempt to restore Browning to his former position as an intellectual leader. J. M. Cohen's *Robert Browning*, published in 1952, is a book in many ways favorable to the poet. It is Cohen's belief that Browning has been rated too low by the latter-day critics and that he is in dire need of revaluation. One point—that of the charges of facile optimism—Cohen is at pains to clarify at the very outset. That Browning was an optimist is quite true, writes Cohen, "But smug or facile he certainly was not."[18] Again, a word of praise is indicated when Cohen calls *A Death in the Desert* "one of the most profound statements of the Protestant standpoint in English poetry, for its certainty

[16]*Ibid.*
[17]"Molinos: The 'Subject of the Day' in *The Ring and the Book*," *PMLA*, LXVII (1952), 308.
[18]Cohen, *Robert Browning*, p. 1.

has also been gained in a struggle, in this case in a struggle against the forces of both dogma and doubt."[19]

But the author of *Robert Browning* is clearly on the side of those who have dispelled what they thought was the myth of the poet-philosopher, blaming the myth largely on Browning's worshipers, although the poet himself is not completely exonerated. One reason for his failure to achieve philosophic stature Cohen praises thus: "Browning was a poet of considerable intellectual ingenuity, but he was not a philosopher; he makes no general statements about man's place in the world."[20] Another fault in Browning's thought is his "faint comprehension of the Catholic attitude. For despite his frequent choice of Catholic subjects for many of his greatest poems," writes Cohen, "he has hardly even an average outsider's understanding of Catholicism."[21]

Easter-Day, much praised as a solution to many religious questions, fares no better in the hands of this writer. Discussing it with *Christmas-Eve,* its companion piece, he writes:

> The second of the poems, "Easter Day," is in intention a dispute concerning the way in which man may
>> "At last awake
>> From life, that insane dream we take
>> For waking now."
> But no such inquiry into man's fate is, in fact, attempted; the poem is no more than an argument in which a visionary, of no greater depth of experience than the narrator of "Christmas Eve," is pitted against a sceptic.[22]

This is also the case with *La Saisiaz,* another poem in which Browning speaks for himself. The poem for Cohen is "stronger in its review of the good things of life he had enjoyed than

[19]*Ibid.,* p. 110.
[20]*Ibid.,* p. 6.
[21]*Ibid.,* p. 61.
[22]*Ibid.,* p. 62.

in its statement of philosophical belief," and its "argument is loose and over-wordy . . ."[23] The treatment of *Ferishtah's Fancies* is only slightly less unfriendly, perhaps because in that volume Browning's philosophical pretensions are less extreme. "Deliberately," writes Cohen, "he seems to be limiting his claims, husbanding that minimum of his spiritual resources in which he could ultimately count. There is no affirmation as far-reaching as that of 'Easter Day,' none so positive in its exposition as 'A Death in the Desert.' "[24]

In many ways, Cohen's attitude is a fairly sensible one and represents an attempt to see both sides fully. He will not subscribe to, or in any way support, Browning as a deep and serious thinker, but he will not allow the poet's ill-deserved title of poet-philosopher to disguise his true worth. The author of *Robert Browning* is neither an image breaker nor maker. And to the worshipers and the pundits he leaves this comforting word:

> Browning had indeed a philosophical message, though not one of the kind the Browning society was looking for. The secret, he tells us again and again, is to be found in man's experience, not in abstraction but in the welter and richness, in the violence and colour, in the love and beauty of the world itself.[25]

Like Cohen's *Robert Browning,* Betty Miller's biography, *Robert Browning: A Portrait,* was also published in 1952. The manners of the two biographers, however, differ greatly. Mrs. Miller is concerned almost solely with interpreting psycho-

[23]*Ibid.,* p. 152.

[24]*Ibid.,* p. 162. See also Mr. Cohen's "Seeing Browning Plain," *The Spectator,* CLXXXIX (1952), 637–638, in which the same point is made. This article will be noted as No. 1 in order to distinguish it from a second Cohen wrote under the same title. An account of the repercussion of that notice is given in the text of this chapter.

[25]*Ibid.,* p. 193.

logically the actions which marked Browning's life. She does not, therefore, say a great deal which bears directly on the subject here at hand. The overall effect of her book, nevertheless, is, if anything, to damage Browning's reputation as a serious-minded person whose pronouncements on philosophy, faith, or morals are worthy of attentive and respectful hearing. Depending heavily upon the multitude of letters by, to, and about Browning, and wielding her evidence as though it were a flat-edged palette knife, Mrs. Miller scrapes assiduously away at past portraits of Browning until at the end of her labors we are given a scarred painting of Browning as an insecure, incompetent mama's boy who in one sense was a failure at everything, including his roles as suitor and father. One who accepts Mrs. Miller's skillfully written account can hardly find room in which to fit a reputation as a serious thinker. The few comments that she does make about his thought bear out this contention. In one place, for example, there is the briefest of passing remarks on "the curious intellectual position in which the man born with a 'wolfish hunger after knowledge' found himself in the last years of his life.

> Wholly distrust thy knowledge, then, and trust
> As wholly love allied to ignorance!
> There lies thy truth and safety."[26]

The tone of this statement is one which does not display great respect for the described "intellectual position." A similar attitude of condemnation is reflected in Mrs. Miller's account of Browning's reversal of his position on Shelley, whom he once heartily admired, yet whom he later rejected, especially in begging off from heading the Shelley Society. She writes:

> Incongruously, now, it was on the plea of Shelley's inhumanity, his desertion of Harriet, that he chose to condemn one who all his life had been "as a nerve o'er which do creep the else

[26]Miller, p. 11. The quotation is from *A Pillar at Sebsevah*.

unfelt oppressions of this earth." Incongruously, indeed: for the man who complained of inhumanity in Shelley was the author of *Ferishtah's Fancies:* a work which, in its complacency, its facile evasion of the problem of evil, its cheerful indifference to human society, must have carried dismay into the ranks of the Browning Society itself.[27]

The essential agreement of the attitudes of Mrs. Miller and Mr. Cohen towards Browning as a thinker is displayed in Cohen's review of *Robert Browning: A Portrait* published in *The Spectator* late in 1952. On the whole, the reviewer commends Mrs. Miller's book, describing it as "an excellent book which will be for many years the standard life of the poet." His chief objection is that she has neglected Browning's poetry and his religious beliefs. The comment most pertinent to this study, however, deals more directly with Browning's reputation as a thinker. Writes Cohen:

> ... it is no doubt better to search with Mrs. Miller for the reasons of his weakness than to hymn with the Browning Society and his friend and first biographer, Mrs. Sutherland Orr, his profound philosophical message to the world. For Browning had no deep moral message, and his blustering exterior certainly hid an inner self-dissatisfaction.[28]

Although Betty Miller and J. M. Cohen seemed able to agree that Browning was neither a great teacher nor a deep thinker, this agreement was not universal, as the aftermath of Cohen's review clearly indicates. *The Spectator* for December 19, 1952, carries a letter from a Scots gentleman who evidently could not bear to see Browning's dismissal as a moral teacher go unchallenged. Of this dismissal John L. Hardie writes, "... it is difficult for one of an older generation to accept this dictum, and certainly at the turn of the century it would have been received with amazement and incredulity."

[27]*Ibid.,* p. 270.
[28]Cohen, "Seeing Browning Plain" (No. 1), pp. 637–638.

In a tone of mild reprimand, Hardie reminds his readers that in the 1890's another Scotsman, Sir Henry Jones, had thought well enough of Browning's moral message to write *Browning as a Philosophical and Religious Teacher.* Well nigh inevitable is the mournful and reproaching conclusion, "O tempora! O, mores!"[29]

Cohen was not slow to come to his own defense against Hardie's implications. Two weeks later, January 2, 1953, he replied in a letter to *The Spectator,* a letter which is deserving of quotation because it represents what seems to me an attitude shared by many critics of Browning who wish to give the poet's reputation a firmer base than they can find in his philosophical teachings. Cohen writes to the editor:

> Sir,—in stating in my review that the poet had "no deep moral message," I was combating the attitude of those Browning Society pundits who with F. J. Nettleship demanded on every occasion: "For us today what is the lesson that the poet would teach?" Unlike the Victorians, we do not today look to our poets for moral messages. We do, however, look to them for true emotion and for a scrupulous statement of their own experience. Here Browning offers us a real lesson. It is impossible, nevertheless, in my belief, to go to him for guidance "in the weightier matters of morality and religion." For here it is the religious teacher and not the poet who is the authority. Nor does this fact seem to me to rob Browning's poetry of any tittle of its greatness.
>
> —Yours faithfully.
>
> J. M. COHEN[30]

The frequency of adverse criticism slackened somewhat after this exchange, but it has not ceased. Perhaps the most important adverse commentary is that of Hoxie N. Fairchild in the fourth volume of his series *Religious Trends in English*

[29]Hardie, "Seeing Browning Plain," *The Spectator,* CLXXXIX (1952), 848.

[30]"Seeing Browning Plain," *The Spectator,* CXC (1953), 16.

Poetry.[31] Fairchild is an enemy of what he calls romanticism in religious poetry, and he does not approve subjective feeling as a sole basis for belief. As a result, he finds in Browning a "lack of aesthetic, ethical, and spiritual discrimination" which "largely justifies Santayana's celebrated condemnation of Browning's 'barbarism.' "[32] Fairchild is no one-sided reader of Browning, but he does not subscribe to the thesis that Browning's philosophy was itself particularly significant. Instead he finds that the *Asolando* epilogue—and, by implication, many of Browning's philosophic or religious utterances —merely gave the reading public "an illusion of spiritual uplift."[33]

One can infer from *Robert Browning and the Babylonian Woman* my opinion that there were certain matters about which Browning was unable to think objectively. The scope of this essay, however, is so narrow that general conclusions about Browning's philosophy were out of place.[34]

Other minor criticisms of Browning's thought have centered on the ring metaphor in *The Ring and the Book* and on *The Statue and the Bust.* A lively, if informal, symposium on the first matter was carried on in the pages of *The Victorian Newsletter* in 1959 and 1960. Paul Cundiff defended Browning from the charge that he did not know that he was interpreting and idealizing the "facts" of the Roman murder case, but Donald Smalley disagreed, arguing that Browning really believed he had not tampered with the facts in any way.[35]

---

[31](New York, 1957), pp. 132–167.

[32]*Ibid.,* p. 155.

[33]*Ibid.,* pp. 166–167.

[34]Boyd Litzinger, *Robert Browning and the Babylonian Woman* (*Baylor Browning Interests,* No. 19 [Waco, Texas, 1962]).

[35]Paul A. Cundiff, "Robert Browning: 'Our Human Speech,' " *The Victorian Newsletter,* No. 15 (Spring, 1959), 1–9; Donald Smalley, "Browning's View of Fact in *The Ring and the Book,*" *VNL,* No. 16 (Fall, 1959), 1–9; and Cundiff, "Robert Browning: 'Indisputably Fact,' " *VNL,* No. 17 (Spring, 1960), 7–11.

Several writers have commented briefly upon *The Statue and the Bust* in recent years. John Bayley has used this poem as an example of Browning's failure when attempting to add morals to his poems, and has called the effort "not so satisfactory."[36] William O. Raymond, on the other hand, reads the moral as consistent with Browning's belief that evil will be transmuted into good and therefore that the passivity of the lovers is more damaging to them than an active sin of adultery would have been.[37] I have disagreed with Professor Raymond, feeling that Browning simply had not thought out the moral and ethical consequences of his thesis and was therefore inconsistent.[38]

If Browningites could take little joy in the continuing stream of adverse criticism, they could still find room for hope; a number of works in praise of Browning as a thinker have also reached print since 1950. Certainly they could take comfort from Dallas Kenmare's *Ever a Fighter,* published in 1952. What future generations would think of the poet if they had only the biographies by Kenmare and Mrs. Miller to go by is a matter of most interesting speculation, for two books could scarcely be less alike. One finds it difficult to remember that the two authors are writing about the same man. In short, *Ever a Fighter* is wholly adulatory and would seem more appropriate in the setting of the 1890's than the 1950's.

Justifying a new study of Browning, Kenmare writes that "the wide sweep of his thought, the depth of his understanding, the apparent contradictions of his passionate mind—for Browning was nothing if not a *passionate* thinker—all demand

[36]*The Romantic Survival* (London, 1957), p. 34.

[37]"Browning's 'The Statue and the Bust,' " *University of Toronto Quarterly,* XXVIII (1959), 233–249.

[38]"Browning's 'The Statue and the Bust' Once More," *Studies in Honor of John C. Hodges and Alwin Thaler* (Knoxville, Tenn., 1961), pp. 87–92.

close and prolonged thought and study."[39] Further, he finds
that "no other English poet is so consistently and continuously
Christian as Browning,"[40] who came with "a profound message which works to remedy not the situation responsible for
our immediate ills, but the *causes* underlying and thus produc-
ing the situation itself."[41] Kenmare's enthusiastic approach to
Browning, especially the praise of Browning's joyful exultation
in every aspect of life and his apparent delight in the energies
of it, is quite obvious throughout the book, but never is the
evangelical fervor of *Ever a Fighter* more clearly shown than
when the author exhorts the reader to a quick acceptance
of this philosophy. Kenmare fairly seems to shout:

> ... we must return to the life poets and quickly, if civilization
> is to be saved. Shelley, Whitman, William Blake, Robert
> Browning—always their message is Life and the wonder and
> joy of life, the sheer miracle of being alive at all.[42]

Kenmare continued this support of Browning a year later in
the pages of *The Contemporary Review*.[43] As though to
counteract a superficial view in certain recent books, Kenmare
writes:

> It is a fact well worth remembering that hitherto literally
> hundreds, both in England and in other countries, have been
> published, all, without exception, evoking a singularly con-
> sistent picture of the great English poet, the picture of a man
> of genius whose actual life did indeed approach the stature of

[39]*Ever a Fighter: A Modern Approach to the Work of Robert
Browning* (London, 1952), p. 11.
[40]*Ibid.*, p. 13.
[41]*Ibid.*, p. 21.
[42]*Ibid.*, p. 54.
[43]"Robert Browning," *The Contemporary Review*, CLXXXIV
(1953), 355–359.

his poetry, and that the majority by far were the testimonies of those who knew him personally.[44]

An oblique reference in this passage to Mrs. Miller seems to me nearly unmistakable, for it is her book on Browning which gives one a picture of the poet absolutely the opposite of the one Kenmare has adduced as being a nearly universal picture of Browning. In another statement, as though in answer to Cohen, Kenmare adds a word of praise for Nettleship, and, finally, pays tribute to Browning's philosophy of life by writing that the poet, "like Albert Schweitzer, feels reverence for life like a passion."[45]

As one might well expect, no other writer in the Fifties has subscribed to the extent that Kenmare has to praising Browning as a teacher or leader. A few instances can be found, however, in which writers have either praised Browning's thought or have put it into such contexts that praise accrues to it. Among these writers we might mention Bennett Weaver, Joseph E. Duncan, and William O. Raymond.[46] The effect of Weaver's article is to exonerate Browning from the charge of unthinking or absolute optimism on the grounds that the poet frequently employed the device of satire in his poetry. Writes Weaver:

> One who believes that "God's in his heaven—/All's right with the world" has no occasion to write satire. But Browning is aware of evil in the world, and his satire ranges from the jolly "Sibrandus" to the sadly ironic "Toccata." Whatever denies life is open to his attack; and in treating his subjects

[44]*Ibid.*, p. 355.
[45]*Ibid.*, p. 359.
[46]Bennett Weaver, "A Primer Study in Browning's Satire," *College English*, XIV (1952), 76–81; Joseph E. Duncan, "The Intellectual Kinship of John Donne and Robert Browning," *SP*, L (1953), 81–100; William O. Raymond, " 'The Jewelled Bow': A Study in Browning's Imagery and Humanism," *PMLA*, LXX (1955), 115–131.

his artistry is subtle, adequate, variously satisfying. His way is the way of the dramatist; his purpose to show vanity her own feature; "Yet malice never [is] his aim."[47]

Duncan adds to Browning's reputation less by directness than by association, for the purpose of his article, published in 1953, is to demonstrate "The Intellectual Kinship of John Donne and Robert Browning." But Duncan is more interested in showing similarities and possible indebtednesses of the younger man to the older than he is in re-establishing Browning as a thinker. Praise is nearest approached in such passages as these: "While Browning's approach to analogies was more logical than that of many of the earlier nineteenth-century poets, it was characteristically more subjective and intuitive than that of the seventeenth-century metaphysicals,"[48] and

> Although Browning's figures probably reflect in some measure his belief in a correspondence between the material and the spiritual, they apparently are not a product of the poet's perception and conception of the universe to the extent that Donne's are. His metaphors probably depend more on sheer ingenuity—and less on belief—than those of Donne.[49]

Duncan's relegating Browning to the subordinate clauses in these passages keeps the conjunction of Donne and Browning from reflecting much credit upon the latter, and Browning fares a bit better when Duncan writes that both poets "had a limited faith in reason, but took pleasure in setting forth ingenious arguments to which they partly subscribed—but which they completely transcended."[50]

William O. Raymond, writing in 1955, concentrates more upon demonstrating Browning's Christian humanism than on

[47]Weaver, p. 81.
[48]Duncan, p. 86.
[49]*Ibid.*, p. 98.
[50]*Ibid.*, p. 90.

attempting to re-establish the poet as a thinker. "Browning's philosophy of life," he writes, "with its deep sense of human experience as poised between the absolute and the relative, is reinforced by his religious belief, the profound influence of the spirit and tenets of Christianity."[51] Browning's concept of intellectual knowledge, writes Raymond, is that of the sceptic; but, he adds, "Browning's sceptical theory of knowledge never invalidates the evidence of his heart that God and man are in communion through the sovereign instrumentality of love."[52] Raymond finally finds Browning's theory of development at the bottom of his theory of life when he writes:

> It is Browning's consciousness that the development of a soul on earth can be achieved only by the fashioning of it in the warp and woof of the colored strands of human experience which underlies his philosophy of life and imparts warmth and realism to his poetry.[53]

Two other writers in this period have treated Browning the thinker with respect. F. E. L. Priestley's "A Reading of *La Saisiaz*" is longer on interpretation than on judgment, but it is carefully done and suggests that Browning's thought was deeper than many believe. Priestley argues that natural reticence prevented the poet from exposing the depths of his faith and doubt to the public, that Browning was a kind of Blougram—using arguments as a sort of fence-play, but having "deeper grounds of faith." If critics have found unsatisfying the argument for life-after-death which informs *La Saisiaz*, Priestley holds that the poet's real faith

> was not the loose and simple chain the poem presents, with its successive links of postulates conceded; but was stronger, more

[51]Raymond, " 'The Jewelled Bow,' " p. 117.
[52]*Ibid.*, p. 123.
[53]*Ibid.*, p. 131.

tangled, and included very different sorts of links, particularly where it reached the grave.[54]

In 1956, and again in 1959, Kenneth L. Knickerbocker took up the cudgels in Browning's behalf by controverting two adverse critics—Richard D. Altick and George Santayana. Professor Knickerbocker obviously wishes to re-establish no Browning cult, but just as obviously he believes that Browning was a sounder poet than recent critics have made him out to be. In "A Tentative Apology for Browning" Knickerbocker cuts cleverly at weak assumptions, made by certain writers, that the Browning marriage was essentially unhappy, that Browning suffered from an embittering sense of failure, and that Browning's "palpable excess of health" (Professor Altick's phrase) argues an underlying malady. A passage in which Knickerbocker comments on this last assumption will illustrate his *reductio*:

> If Browning who professed to be healthy was in reality ill, was Carlyle, let us say, who professed to be chronically dyspeptic, in reality well? Did Keats die of too much health and was Milton really blind? If Freudian interpretations work in one direction only, then the healthy are sick and the sick are sick too. A parlous state.[55]

Perhaps the point at which this critic joins issue most pertinently for this study is his examination of the process by which Browning rejected knowledge, a sore point with Jones, Santayana, and many others. Knickerbocker does not disapprove of Browning's intellectual agnosticism, holding that the poet "*thought* his way into a distrust of thinking—as many a

---

[54]"A Reading of *La Saisiaz*," *University of Toronto Quarterly*, XXV (1955), 59.

[55]"A Tentative Apology for Browning," *Tennessee Studies in Literature*, I (1956), 77.

man has done before and since."[56] In short, Professor Knickerbocker is not prepared to agree with those who judge Browning's philosophy by their own yardsticks. "There are plenty of
systems," he writes, "and none of them satisfactory."[57]

Thus we can anticipate his attack on Santayana, a man who
thought he *had* a satisfactory system by which to judge Browning. Knickerbocker argues that by temperament and temper
Santayana was naturally hostile to Browning as both poet and
thinker. It is therefore unfair to judge him by philosophic
standards to which the poet never subscribed, and, indeed,
Browning would likely have been a poorer poet had he accepted the comparatively ascetic assumptions which underlie
Santayana's "The Poetry of Barbarism."[58] It ought to be noted
that Professor Knickerbocker has announced his intention of
pursuing further this defense of Browning against his adverse
critics.[59]

The favorable comments of Raymond and Cundiff have
been alluded to earlier in this chapter, and it remains only
to be said that no one since 1959 has given Browning the
thinker much favorable attention.

Besides these critics who have sided either with or against
Browning as a thinker, the last decade or so has seen printed
the articles and books of a number of people who have neither
added to nor detracted from the poet's reputation for serious
thought but who have not, on the other hand, failed to treat
or to notice it. Such critics keep before their readers the re-
minder that Browning has been much praised and blamed for
his philosophy and message.

As one might expect, these writers quite frequently bring
up the matter of Browning's optimism. Margaret Willy, for

[56]*Ibid.*, p. 81.
[57]*Ibid.*
[58]"Robert Browning: A Modern Reappraisal," *Tennessee Studies in
Literature*, IV (1959), 1–11.
[59]"A Tentative Apology," p. 81.

example, calls Browning an indomitable optimist, one to whom all things "conspired positively for good."[60] In even such a searching poem as *La Saisiaz* she finds his optimism maintained by a "concluding note . . . if necessarily not of knowledge, at least of a sustaining hope."[61] The most useful discussion of Browning's optimism published during this period is to be found in Professor Kenneth L. Knickerbocker's introduction to the Modern Library edition of *The Selected Poetry of Robert Browning* (1951). After showing that the nature of the four episodes of *Pippa Passes* displays an optimism that "can hardly be called flagrant Pollyannaism,"[62] Professor Knickerbocker directs the student to the concluding lines of *Apparent Failure,* lines which declare Browning's belief that man is morally irresponsible. The editor writes that "This is surely a onesided antinomianism which implies that man has 'God's warrant' to protect him from any ultimate responsibility for his own actions. Here, I think, is the best evidence of Browning's confirmed optimism."[63] A similar explanation is that given four years later by Thomas Marc Parrott and Robert B. Martin who described Browning's optimism "as a belief that an ever-present, beneficent power rules the world."[64] Jerome Buckley, studying the literary culture of the Victorian period, singles out this optimistic conception of the cosmos when he writes:

> The major voice of aspiration was inevitably one that had mastered the logic of ebullient acceptance; it was Robert

[60]"The Indomitable Optimist: Robert Browning," *Life Was Their Cry* (London, 1950), p. 196.

[61]*Ibid.*, p. 193.

[62]*The Selected Poetry of Robert Browning* (New York, 1951), p. xvi. Judging from the date of this introduction, one might conclude that Betty Miller's book and Richard Altick's article stimulated Professor Knickerbocker's later and stronger defenses of Browning.

[63]*Ibid.*, p. xviii.

[64]*A Companion to Victorian Literature* (New York, 1955), p. 168.

Browning who attained the immediate assent, far readier than
Goethe's, far easier than Tennyson's.[65]

Browning's popularity, Buckley further explains, is due in part
to the poet's "own brand of Christian Platonism," by which
he "postulated a solution to the problem of evil which was
acceptable to many Victorians responsive to various idealistic
philosophies."[66]

Unlike most of these writers, E. D. H. Johnson sees Browning in conflict, rather than agreement, with his own age. This
opposition he feels is shown principally in Browning's doctrine
of imperfection and in his rejection of the intellect. Johnson
writes that in the face of rising rationalism and faith in progress, "By a constant advocacy of intuitive over rational knowledge Browning took over the anti-intellectualism of the
Romantics and pushed it in the direction of pure primitivism."[67]
He writes of an aspect of the doctrine of imperfection that is
seldom touched upon when he says that it "has anti-social
implications," for the "belief holds that an individual's first
and highest obligation is to fulfill his own being, regardless
of consequences."[68] Finally, the matters of intuition and imperfection are drawn together to show the poet in revolt
against his times. Johnson writes that "By his celebration of
intuitive being Browning sets his face against the Benthamite
psychology, with its teaching that man is a knowable mecha-
nism and hence capable of being tinkered into perfection."[69]
Thus, although Johnson does not give heady praise to Browning the thinker, the poet is given credit for more intellectual
courage than many mid-century critics are willing to grant
him.

[65]*The Victorian Temper: A Study in Literary Culture* (Cambridge, Mass., 1951), p. 89.
[66]*Ibid.,* p. 90.
[67]*The Alien Vision of Victorian Poetry* (Princeton, 1952), p. 92.
[68]*Ibid.,* pp. 94–95.
[69]*Ibid.,* p. 216.

H. C. Duffin's *Amphibian: A Reconsideration of Browning* (1956) seems to have grown out of a certain enthusiasm for Browning, but it takes a balanced view of Browning as a thinker. Duffin devotes a substantial section to Browning's philosophical poems, but he makes no attempt to glorify them. Browning's optimism he calls "an uncertain quantity," his philosophy a "Sursum corda" supported "by arguments that have no meaning for us."[70] In his summing up, Mr. Duffin places himself with the moderates: "Interesting as we may find his religious and ethical views," he writes, "they are of permanent value only when he has arrived at them by poetic intuition."[71]

John Bryson's booklet in the *Writers and Their Work* series continues this tradition of playing down the philosophy by complaining of the "over-zealous worship" of the Browning-ites, by repeating the now-old bromide that Browning was no easy optimist, and by locating the poet's obscurity not in "the abstruse nature of his thought" but in "a quick, abrupt way of thinking which does make special demands on the reader."[72]

The evidence of this chapter, then, is that the general critical judgment in recent years has continued against Browning as a thinker, but that a significant body of critics may feel that the judgment has been too severe. It would seem that the game of beating the philosophic horse is waning and that a counter-reaction is beginning to set in. No one, I believe, would predict a groundswell of support for Browning's philosophy, but it would appear that Browning's reputation as a thinker has risen a degree or two in the last decade.

[70]*Amphibian*, pp. 252–253.
[71]*Ibid.*, p. 291.
[72]*Robert Browning* (London, 1959), pp. 7–8.

Mine was the better way, I do calmly believe, for at this moment
I feel as everybody does who has worked—*"in vain"? no matter,*
if the work was real. ☙ BROWNING TO ALFRED DOMETT

SOME CONCLUSIONS

SO FAR AS I KNOW, THIS STUDY IS
the first to attempt a full sketch of the critics' treatment of
Browning as a thinker. The findings herein reported offer a
starting point for much-needed further investigation. For
example, this work ought to be of use in an evaluation of the
effects the changing times have had on Browning's reputation
with critics: whether much of the adverse criticism directed
against him does not in reality represent a reaction more
against the indiscriminate Browningites than against Browning, whether present-day attitudes towards the dependability
of intuition as a guide to action have changed so markedly
since Browning's death as to have had an adverse effect
on his reputation as a thinker, and whether the critics have
not oversimplified Browning's beliefs. The list could be extended indefinitely to include, for instance, the validity of the
Freudian approach to Browning's poetry and life, Browning's
proper place in relation to nineteenth-century thought, and
revaluations of Browning's statements on the matters of love,
evil, and progress. For such inquiries and many others of like
nature, this study may prove of interest.

It has been seen that Browning's reputation for serious
thought was at a high level during the decade following his
death in 1889. He had gained a large reading public during
his last twenty-five years, and his poetic utterances during
the last two decades of his life had become more and more
philosophic in tone and treatment. His death, coinciding

156

precisely with the publication of *Asolando*, increased his fame as a thinker; as has been shown, much of the eulogizing which followed the poet's demise was devoted to Browning's "message," his stature as a philosopher and religious teacher. The *Epilogue* to that final volume helped no little in the spreading of his reputation. Its stirring "Fight ever—there as here!" was interpreted as a *vade mecum* and became the accepted ending for an article or book on Browning.

From another point of view, it is possible to surmise that Browning's death may have had something to do with the silence of the adverse critics, if many did exist. Certainly the critical climate of the 1890's would not have permitted a warm acceptance of anti-Browning propaganda.

The flourishing English Browning Society likewise had its effect on Browning's reputation as a thinker, for its members did not cease praising Browning's philosophy either among themselves or to whatever audience would listen to them. The influence of the Society and its numerous counterparts in America and elsewhere was extensive, and this semi-organized bloc did much to spread Browning's fame as a philosopher in verse. On the other hand, the sometimes fatuous productions of the Browningites gave the adverse critics materials which were to be turned to use, most unfairly, against the poet himself.

During the last decade of the nineteenth century, the two aspects of Browning's thought which most often found favor with the critics were the poet's optimism and his religious views. Browning's optimism could never have appealed to a Thomas Hardy or a Santayana, but Browning's fame as a philosopher was not dependent in the least upon the support of such intellectual luminaries. For Browning was himself no intellectual of the brooding or ascetic sort, and his sympathies were farther from the Jeremiahs and the conservatives than from a middle class which found real value in optimism. At any rate, during the Nineties a considerable number of articulate readers of Browning were enthusiastic enough about his message to bring it to the attention of a wide audience. Browning's religious message also appealed to many readers during the 1890's, thus forming another principal base from which his reputation as a thinker reached great heights during that decade. Many found in Browning's poems an unshaken belief in the existence of an all-loving God, the immortality of the soul, and the divinity of Christ. They approved also his obvious dislike of Catholicism, his scorn of the rationalists and the historical critics of the Bible. There can be little doubt that Browning's reputation as a thinker was enhanced by the praise offered him because of his ability to express his religious ideals in good poetry.

The magnitude of Browning's reputation as a philosopher during the *fin de siècle* is all the more apparent when one considers the scarcity of adverse comment during the decade. The dissenters formed a small body indeed; the matters chosen for adverse comment were, on the whole, quite minor. Certainly the effect of the few criticisms aimed against the poet was infinitely less than that worked by the favorable criticism. A notable exception is *Browning as a Philosophical and Religious Teacher,* in which Henry Jones found Browning's moral message as well as his general philosophy seriously marred by contradictions which seemed only too apparent in the poet's statements about the existence of evil and the validity of human knowledge. It would seem, however, that the force of Jones's objections was not felt strongly during the Nineties, for Browning's reputation as a thinker remained unshaken as the new century dawned.

The years 1900–1909 saw that reputation still flourishing heartily, although perhaps not so heartily as in the 1890's. Interest continued to focus on what the critics judged praiseworthy in Browning's thought, with optimism and religious faith still occupying the center of attention. General statements about the poet's intellectual depth, his subtlety, and his wide knowledge of the human soul continued to play a large part. The London Browning Society had become defunct, it is true, but the activities of other Browning groups seem to have proceeded without abatement. Whatever inspirational value Browning's death had supplied in the previous ten-year span was pretty well dissipated by the first years of the new century. In addition, there was active during the first years of this century a small but sharp element of dissent, led by the criticisms of John Robertson and George Santayana. Their attacks, however, seem to have had little immediate effect on Browning's reputation as a serious thinker. Although both writers were highly critical of Browning's thinking, Santayana's criticism was the more damning one, for he struck at the very base of much of Browning's popularity as a thinker : the poet's robust and enthusiastic acceptance of life as he found it. This approach to a philosophy of life Santayana condemned as "barbaric," lacking in spirituality, in restraint, in self-control, and in self-denial. Nevertheless, Santayana's objections went largely unnoticed, and the close of this decade found very little criticism at work against the poet's reputation as a philosopher and moral influence.

If anything, the years 1910–1919 saw Browning's reputation as a thinker rise to a height slightly above its place in the preceding decade but still somewhat below the mark reached in the 1890's. The great impetus given to the favorable criticism during this decade was, of course, the centenary observation of Browning's birth. The literature printed in 1912 bulked large and is, perhaps, exceeded only by the many writings called forth by Browning's death. The steady flow of favorable comment remained so strong in this decade that the unfavorable critics did not venture many comments of their own.

The 1920's, however, saw the great shift in critical opinion concerning Browning's thought. Browning's admirers were still strong in the Twenties, but the mid-years of the decade found a sudden cooling-off on the part of the critics; the lessening number of favorable comments is in a sense inversely proportional to the increasing strength of Browning's critical foes. The post-war disillusionment had finally reached the literary critics, and they found Browning's robustness hollow. Optimism had become unfashionable in the wastelands of the Lost Generation, and Browning's religious views were simply being looked upon with indifference. Or—just as possibly—the praise of Browning's thought, having been poured forth in great volume for some twenty-five years, had spent itself, allowing the inevitable reaction to set in. In any case, by the end of the decade the unfavorable criticism held sway and Browning's reputation as a thinker began its sharp drop.

The 1930's and 1940's found Browning's reputation as a thinker sunk to a low level despite the fact that scholarly work on Browning went forward at an accelerated pace. The critics presented a wide range of objections, making charges of diverse natures; for example, that Browning failed to take part in the intellectual life of his time, that his optimism was facile and ill-founded, and, inevitably, that he placed too great a dependence on intuition and not enough upon the intellect. Browning's supporters, with a few exceptions like Edwin Mims, failed to come to his defense, and as a result scorn for Browning's thought became in these decades quite as fashionable as admiration for it had been during the preceding years. It is almost as though the supporters of Browning's thought had abandoned the field completely and had left the adverse critics in full control.

Since 1950 there has been a slight change in the critical temperature, a change in Browning's favor. This, however, is due not so much to such writers as Dallas Kenmare, whose adulatory book will hardly find favor with critical readers, as to vigorous efforts on the part of the scholars to build a firmer base for the formation of new judgments about Browning. To be sure, there is very little praise of Browning as a thinker during the early years of this period; it is equally certain that Browning's reputation as a thinker has been in no way enhanced by the severe attacks of such writers as Richard Altick and Betty Miller. And yet the critics since 1950 seem less intent than their predecessors upon image-breaking, perhaps because the images have all been broken, perhaps because there is a realization that the adverse critics have moved almost as far to one extreme as the Browning coterie had toward their own.

This study does not show, however, that there is any great revival of interest in Browning as a thinker, nor does it show that the future is likely to rebuild Browning's reputation for serious thought. There is, on the other hand, this thought to be considered: since it is obvious that the times have had an influence on criticism of Browning's thought, there is the possibility that a time in the future may favor Browning's intuitive approach to a philosophy of life. There is some indication at the present—in the work of K. L. Knickerbocker, for example—that the critics will adjust their opinions of Browning's thought slightly upward. But it seems almost certain that there will be no more philosopher's bays for Browning.

A glance at the quality of the criticism produced by the two extreme camps will show clearly why Browning's reputation as a thinker waned. The favorable critics, glorying in the fine religious sentiments of *Rabbi Ben Ezra* and *Saul,* concluded that the author of such poems was therefore a philosopher. They refused to recognize, on the whole, any contradictions in Browning's dicta; and, worst of all, they produced praise all too often vague and unsatisfying, occasionally fatuous and adulatory in the extreme. The unfavorable critics, on the other hand, have been unwilling to accept Browning's philosophy simply because of the religious and moral support he seems to have given to a segment of his reading public. They have concentrated on the contradictions they found in Browning's verse, and the adverse critics have been comparatively concise in their arguments and thorough in their analyses of Browning's thought. Too frequently, however, these critics have aimed their attacks at the excesses of the Browningites and have ignored the important matter of a systematic study of Browning himself.

Among the critical faults common to those who have discussed Browning's philosophy, two—enthusiasm and prejudice—are outstanding. The critics have found in Browning what they hoped, what they were prepared, to find. The generations of pious folk, seeking intellectual support for their received philosophical positions, glorified Browning as the spokesman for their party, called him the articulator of their dumb faith. There is no doubt in my mind that Browning's sustained popularity was due in large measure to the workings of this party, nor is there any doubt that—consciously or not—Browning filled an essential spiritual need for these people. They were not objective scholars either by profession or by inclination and their faith, if deep, was eclectic. Those who wrote out of, or for, this group had to pick and choose from Browning's poems such passages as nourished their beliefs; they ignored or explained away those poems and passages which they could not fit into their picture of Browning as a middle-class, optimistic, evangelical Christian philosopher.

The iconoclasts, the unbelievers, the agnostics, and the sceptics associated Browning too closely with his supporters. They saw him as a representative of philistine religion and morality, used him as a horrible example, branded him a philosophic pretender; and of his exposed pretensions they made clubs with which to beat the dead horse of nineteenth-century optimism. Thomas Hardy's comment on Browning's grocer-like mentality is clever, but like many other clever things it is unjust and will not bear the light of objective judgment.

Lovers of poetry and *belles lettres* in general have simply deplored—and with good reason—the poet's philosophic excursions. And few indeed are the literary critics willing to defend or discuss what Browning wrote after *The Ring and*

the Book. The compilers of anthologies and selections of poetry mostly ignore the later poems or, at best, give them a de-
ceptive nod by reprinting *Summum Bonum* and an epilogue
or two. Indeed it is not too much to say that the purely literary men have never supported Browning's claim to the philosopher's bays, and that theirs has been a criticism for art's
sake.

And what of the philosophers? Ordinarily, they have been
unable to approach Browning dispassionately. Henry Jones
may well be the sole exception. The philosophers have regarded Browning as an unwelcome intruder, a philosophical
illiterate rushing fearlessly and foolishly into matters of which
he was profoundly ignorant. They have often labored under
the disadvantage of an imperfect knowledge of Browning,
and one gets the impression—most dramatically in the case
of Santayana—that half their scorn is directed against the
Browningites, not against the poet.

Beyond all this lies a further fact, one which has significantly influenced the whole problem. No critic has, as yet,
documented his case for or against Browning with what must
be called, for want of a better phrase, sufficient and satisfying
evidence. Some critics (Jones, again, the best of the lot) have
attempted rather full analyses of Browning's thought; a good
number of others have obviously brought a deep knowledge
of the poet to bear upon their theses. Nevertheless, no critic
has as yet attacked the problem with all the scholarly and
critical equipment available. Recent critics (like Raymond
and myself in our discussions of *The Statue and the Bust*)
who have addressed themselves to specific points, problems,
poems, and proofs, have been able to do little more than
sketch broad outlines and imply larger views. Many recent
writers have been concerned with refuting or correcting the
accounts of earlier writers and have necessarily restricted
themselves to specific topics.

The disadvantages under which writers at the turn of the

century labored have by and large disappeared. Earlier critics in this century worked under the dual hardships of general disinterest in things Victorian and of incorrect and incomplete biographical information, worked often without a full knowledge of even the primary materials from which general conclusions could safely be drawn. But the study of Browning has come a long way in the past few decades, and we are approaching the day when these disadvantages will have been substantially overcome. We have begun to reach what seems to be a proper aesthetic distance from the nineteenth century, certain Browning materials have been recovered (one thinks at once of the Chatterton essay), more facts about the poet (the Ashburton episode, for example) have been brought to light, new letters and sounder editions of old ones have been published, a fine bibliography and stimulating new approaches towards the man and his poems have come to us, and the revival of interest in the Victorians has stimulated the minds of a good many sound scholars. Of course, we need a great deal more. Many letters remain unpublished, a definitive biography remains unwritten, textual studies and a new edition of the poems are badly needed.

Time will see these needs fulfilled, and things are looking up. There exists today neither a pro-Browning nor an anti-Browning cult. The poet has recovered from the twin ailments of extreme praise and blame, and the time is nearer when objectively critical evaluations can be made. And these evaluations will have to take into consideration Browning's thought. If this study has done nothing else, it has shown that many critics have not been criticizing, but reacting. The treatment of Browning as a thinker has often been visceral rather than intellectual. It is obvious that the Browningites found the poet's philosophy emotionally satisfying and that their proselytizing efforts set in motion an opposite—and equally emotional—reaction. We can only hope that future estimates will be calmer.

It will not do, however, to follow the tendency of the critics who would simply ignore Browning's philosophy. We must properly take it into consideration in any balanced judgment of Browning—not merely because his followers called him a philosopher, but more because the thought-content of his work is an important part of his poetry. It cannot be safely ignored. It is impossible to make a balanced judgment of *The Ring and the Book* or even *Rabbi Ben Ezra*—not to speak of *Ferishtah's Fancies*—without judging the philosophic assumptions underlying the poetry. On the other hand, the philosophy is only a part, and to judge the poet by his thought alone will prove a perilous course.

The balanced judgment for which we hope is complicated, for Browning did his best to hide himself in his poems. "Some think, Creation's meant to show him forth:/I say it's meant to hide him all it can"—Blougram in this case might (as long as one does not read too far) have been speaking for the poet and his works. The problem of distinguishing the subjective beliefs of a poet who was professedly objective is a difficult, but not an impossible, one. It will be a tedious task requiring persistence, patience, and a philosophic turn of mind. The critic will have to begin with an absolutely full knowledge of the poems. Both his stomach and his eyes will have to be strong, unless he has a taste for poems like *Prince Hohenstiel-Schwangau* and *Red Cotton Night-Cap Country* and owns the Centenary edition. (There will be a special punishment in hell for the publishers of one-volume, double-column "complete" works: they will have to collate an infinite number of such editions by flickering fires in sulfurous cubicles.) Mastering the poems will be only the first step. This ideal critic will then sift fact from fancy in the biographies and memoirs, read between the lines of letters and second-hand reports, and draw conclusions as to what Browning actually did think about this topic or that.

He will then have the basic equipment necessary for the

next task, that of piercing the dramatic veil of the poems. Working from the so-called autobiographical poems to the so-called objective ones, he will develop, both topically and chronologically, a sound notion of Browning's philosophy of life. At this point he will be prepared for critical judgment —a triple task. First he will evaluate the philosophy as objectively as he can. Next, he will judge it in the context of the poems themselves. Finally, he will judge it in the larger context of the thought and poetry of Browning's time. It is a taxing job, one which will not be eased by the sure knowledge that every Browning scholar will disagree with his conclusions wholly or in part.

It will be noted that I do not recommend to our critic of the future a systematic study of earlier commentary. If he takes the accepted way of citing every earlier explorer of these thickets—or worse, of disputing the conclusions of every predecessor—neither he nor his readers will ever find the way out of the maze. A footnote-less work of scholarship may be impossible in this case, but our scholar will do well to cite only primary sources. Browning students will bless him, even when they disagree with him, if he simply says, *Here I stand.*

Will the game be worth the candle, a very long and expensive candle? To paraphrase Browning's question, Why take the scholar's way to prove so little? It will be worth the while if humanistic study has any value at all. We are dealing with a major poet, and we cannot ignore the man. There is a scale of values in which poetry—and sometimes, it seems, even man—counts for nothing. But some of us do not subscribe to these values or worry greatly about the disdain of those who do; and so we must find poetry, and philosophy, the blend of the two and the criticism of both, worth attention "if precious be the soul of man to man."

Perhaps there can be no real conclusion to the argument over Browning's merits as a thinker; perhaps the matter will merely be let drop. Certainly subjective judgments will continue to have—as they have had in the past—a great part in the assessment. For those who like their philosophies based upon intuitions or who find all philosophies equally fallible, Browning will be an acceptable if not an excellent thinker. For those who like their philosophies more formal and consistent, who believe that certitude can be attained through intellectual processes, and who find systematic philosophies superior to other varieties, Browning will not qualify as an important thinker.

The final evaluation of Browning's stature as a thinker is yet to be done. This outline of the course of his decline may serve as an aid to those who are willing to attempt a reassessment.

ACKNOWLEDGMENTS

I AM GRATEFUL FOR THE OPPORTU-
nity to thank those who have helped me prepare this book.
Its existence is owed, first of all, to Professor Kenneth L.
Knickerbocker—teacher, colleague, and friend—whose interest in Browning first stimulated my own. I owe much to his
encouragement over the years, and my debt is not repaid by
this note. My debt to other Browning scholars is recorded
on every page of this book and deserves to be acknowledged
outside the footnotes. Professor Donald Smalley gave the
manuscript a careful, critical reading and so helped to reduce
the number of errors in it.

The editors of *Tennessee Studies in Literature* and *Cithara:
Essays in the Judeo-Christian Tradition* have permitted me
to reprint material (now parts of the first two chapters) which
first appeared in the pages of their journals. The President
and Vice-President of St. Bonaventure University—Very Rev.
Francis W. Kearney, O.F.M., and Rev. Cornelius A. Welch,
O.F.M.—supplied practical assistance in the form of pay-
ments to a professional typist.

What a man owes to his wife can neither be expressed
nor repaid in words, but I am happy to record here my
deep indebtedness to Maria Litzinger.

BIBLIOGRAPHY

"A Browning Anniversary." *The Bookman,* XXIII (1906), 590–592.

Abercrombie, Lascelles. "Robert Browning, 1812–1889." *The Great Victorians.* H. J. and Hugh Massingham, eds. New York: Doubleday, Doran and Company, 1932.

Abrahams, Israel. *By-Paths in Hebraic Bookland.* Philadelphia: The Jewish Publication Society of America, 1920.

Altick, Richard D. "The Private Life of Robert Browning." *Yale Review,* XLI (1952), 247–262.

Ariail, J. M. "Is 'Pippa Passes' a Dramatic Failure?" *SP,* XXXVII (1940), 120–129.

Armstrong, A. J. "Browning's Testament of Hope." *The Baylor Bulletin,* XXXVIII (1935), 1–30.

Axson, Stockton. "Browning's Philosophy of Life." *Rice Institute Pamphlet,* XVIII (1931), 181–199.

Bates, Margret Holmes. *Browning Critiques.* Chicago: The Morris Book Shop, 1921.

Batho, Edith C., and Bonamy Dobrée. *The Victorians and After, 1830–1914.* London: The Cresset Press, 1950.

Bayley, John. *The Romantic Survival.* London: Constable and Company, Ltd., 1957.

Beach, Joseph Warren. *The Concept of Nature in Nineteenth-Century English Poetry.* New York: The Macmillan Company, 1936.

Beale, Dorothea. "Christmas Eve." *Literary Studies of Poems, New and Old.* London: George Bell and Son, 1902.

Benn, Alfred William. *The History of English Rationalism in the Nineteenth Century.* London: Longmans, Green and Company, 1906.

Berdoe, Edward, ed. *Browning Studies.* New York: The Macmillan Company, 1895.

Birrell, Augustine. "Robert Browning: An Address Delivered at the Browning Hall Settlement, December 12, 1897." *The Collected Essays and Addresses of the Rt. Hon. Augustine Birrell, 1880–1920.* 3 Vols. London: J. M. Dent and Sons, Ltd., 1922.

B[loomfield]-M[oore], C[lara] J. "Robert Browning." *Lippincott's Magazine,* XLV (1890), 683–691.

Bonner, G. H. "Robert Browning." *The Nineteenth Century and After*, XCVI (1924), 219–227.

"The Bookman's Table." *The Bookman*, II (1895), 535–536.

Bowers, R. H. "Santayana and Browning: A Postscript." *N&Q*, CXCIV (1949), 433–434.

Bradford, Gamaliel, Jr. "Browning and Sainte-Beuve." *North American Review*, CXCI (1910), 488–500.

————. "The Return of the Druses." *Boston Browning Society Papers*. New York: The Macmillan Company, 1897.

Brooke, Stopford A. "Robert Browning." *The Contemporary Review*, LVII (1890), 141–152.

————. *The Poetry of Robert Browning*. New York: Thomas Y. Crowell and Company, 1902.

————. "The Religious Teaching of Browning." *Literary Studies of Poems, New and Old*. London: George Bell and Son, 1902.

Broughton, Leslie N., Clark S. Northup, and Robert Pearsall. *Robert Browning: A Bibliography, 1830–1950*. Ithaca: Cornell University Press, 1953.

"Browning in the Future." *Scribner's Magazine*, XI (1892), 264.

Bruce, Alexander B. *The Moral Order of the World in Ancient and Modern Thought*. New York: Charles Scribner's Sons, 1899.

Bryson, John. *Robert Browning*. London: Longmans, Green and Company, Ltd., 1959.

Buck, Gerhard. "Das Nachleben Robert Brownings in Kritik und Forschung." *Germanisch-Romanische Monatsschrift*, XXI (1933), 207–221.

Buck, Philo M. *The World's Great Age: The Story of a Century's Search for a Philosophy of Life*. New York: The Macmillan Company, 1936.

Buckley, Jerome H. *The Victorian Temper: A Study in Literary Culture*. Cambridge: Harvard University Press, 1951.

Burdett, Osbert. *The Beardsley Period: An Essay in Perspective*. London: John Lane, 1925.

Burt, Emma J. *The Seen and Unseen in Browning*. Oxford: Basil Blackwell, 1923.

Burton, Richard. "Originality in Literature." *The Dial* (1896), 212–214.

Burton, Richard, ed. *Select Poems of Robert Browning*. Boston: D. C. Heath and Company, 1910.

Bush, Douglas. *Mythology and the Romantic Tradition in English Poetry*. Cambridge: Harvard University Press, 1937.

Campbell, Lily Bess. "The Grotesque in the Poetry of Robert Browning." *Bulletin of the University of Texas* ("Humanistic Series," No. 5), XCII (1907).

"Cardinal Newman." *Edinburgh Review*, CCXV (1912), 263–290.

Carpenter, W. Boyd. *The Religious Spirit in the Poets*. London: Isbister and Company, Ltd., 1900.

Cazamian, Louis. *L'Évolution Psychologique et la Litterature en Angleterre (1660–1914)*. Paris: Librairie Felix Alcan, 1920.

————. "Robert Browning." *A History of English Literature*. Emile Legouis and Louis Cazamian, eds. New York: The Macmillan Company, 1935.

Chapman, Edward Mortimer. *English Literature in Account with Religion*. London: Constable and Company, 1910.

Chapman, John Jay. "Robert Browning." *Emerson and Other Essays*. New York: Charles Scribner's Sons, 1898.

Charlton, H. B. "Browning's Ethical Poetry." *Bulletin of the John Rylands Library*, XXVII (1942), 36–69.

————. "Browning as Poet of Religion." *Bulletin of the John Rylands Library*, XXVII (1943), 271–307.

————. "Browning: The Poet's Aim." *Bulletin of the John Rylands Library*, XXII (1938), 98–121.

Chave, Penrhyn. "Philosophy and Poetry." *The Contemporary Review*, CXXX (1926), 212–221.

Chesterton, Gilbert Keith. "Browning and His Ideal." *A Handful of Authors*. Dorothy Collins, ed. New York: Sheed and Ward, 1953.

————. *Robert Browning*. London: Macmillan and Company, 1903.

Chew, Samuel C. *The Nineteenth Century and After*. (Albert C. Baugh, *et al.*, *A Literary History of England*, Vol. IV.) New York: Appleton-Century-Crofts, 1948.

Clark, Kate Upson. "Browning as a Masquer." *Addresses Commemorating the Birth of Robert Browning Delivered Before the New York Browning Society*. New York: n. p., 1912.

Clarke, George Herbert. "Browning and Tennyson: A Browning

Centenary Study." *The Canadian Magazine,* XXXIX (1912), 120–132.

Clarke, Helen A. *Browning and His Century.* New York: Doubleday, Page, and Company, 1912.

————. *Browning's England.* New York: The Baker and Taylor Company, 1908.

Cohen, J. M. *Robert Browning.* London: Longmans, Green and Company, 1952.

————. "Seeing Browning Plain." *The Spectator,* CLXXXIX (1952), 637–638.

————. "Seeing Browning Plain." *The Spectator,* CXC (1953), 16.

Coleridge, Ernest Hartley. "Browning and Wordsworth on 'Intimations of Immortality.' " *The Robert Browning Centenary Celebration.* William C. Knight, ed. London: Smith, Elder and Company, 1912.

Collins, J. Churton. "Browning and Butler." *The Contemporary Review,* XCVIII (1910), 467–476.

————. *The Posthumous Essays of John Churton Collins.* L. C. Collins, ed. London: J. M. Dent and Sons, 1912.

Compton-Rickett, Arthur. *Robert Browning: Humanist.* New York: The Dial Press, 1925.

Conway, Moncure D. *Autobiography: Memoirs and Experiences of Moncure Daniel Conway.* Boston: Houghton Mifflin Company, 1904.

————. "Recollections of Robert Browning." *Nation,* L (1890), 27–28.

Cooke, George Willis. *A Guide-Book to the Poetic and Dramatic Works of Robert Browning.* Boston: Houghton Mifflin Company, 1891.

Coyle, William. "Molinos: The 'Subject of the Day' in *The Ring and the Book.*" *PMLA,* LXVII (1952), 308–314.

Cross, Wilbur Lucius, and Horatio S. Kraus. "Robert Browning." *The New International Encyclopaedia.* 2nd ed. (1922), IV, 46–48.

Crossley, Anthony. "Browning as a Dramatic Poet and Prophet." *The Spectator,* CXLI (1928), 44–46.

Crum, Ralph B. *Scientific Thought in Poetry.* New York: Columbia University Press, 1931.

Cundiff, Paul A. "Robert Browning: 'Indisputably Fact.' " *VNL,* No. 17 (Spring, 1960), 7–11.

Cundiff, Paul A. "Robert Browning: 'Our Human Speech.'" *VNL,* No. 15 (Spring, 1959), 1–9.

Cunliffe, J. W. "Browning's Idealism." *Transactions of the Wisconsin Academy of Sciences, Arts, and Letters,* XVII (1913), 661–681.

————. "Modern Thought in Meredith's Poems." *PMLA,* XXVII (1912), 1–25.

Daniels, Earl. "The Younger Generation Reads Browning and Tennyson." *The English Journal,* XVIII (1929), 653–661.

Dawson, W. J. *The Makers of English Poetry.* New York: Fleming H. Revell Company, 1906.

De Ford, Miriam Allen. "Robert Browning." *British Authors of the Nineteenth Century.* Stanley J. Kunitz and Howard Haycraft, eds. New York: The H. W. Wilson Company, 1936.

De Reul, Paul. "The Art and Thought of Robert Browning." *Rice Institute Pamphlet,* XIII (1926), 227–304.

DeVane, William C. *A Browning Handbook.* 2nd ed. New York: Appleton-Century-Crofts, 1955.

————. *Browning's Parleyings: The Autobiography of a Mind.* New Haven: Yale University Press, 1927.

————. "The Virgin and the Dragon." *Yale Review,* XXXVII (1947), 33–46.

————, and Kenneth L. Knickerbocker, eds. *New Letters of Robert Browning.* New Haven: Yale University Press, 1950.

Dorchester, Daniel. "Browning's Philosophy of Art." *Boston Browning Society Papers.* New York: The Macmillan Company, 1897.

Dowden, Edward. *Robert Browning.* London: J. M. Dent and Company, 1904.

Drachmann, A. G. "Alloy and Gold." *SP,* XXII (1925), 418–424.

Duckworth, F. R. G. *Browning, Background and Conflict.* New York: E. P. Dutton and Company, 1932.

Duffin, Henry Charles. *Amphibian: A Reconsideration of Browning.* London: Bowes and Bowes Publishers, Ltd., 1956.

Duncan, Joseph E. "The Intellectual Kinship of John Donne and Robert Browning." *SP,* L (1953), 81–100.

Dunn, Martha Baker. "The Browning Tonic." *The Atlantic Monthly,* XC (1902), 203–211.

Dunsany, Lord. "Browning Is Blougram." *The Nineteenth Century and After,* CXXXIX (1946), 175–177.

Ealand, F. *Sermons from Browning.* London: S. C. Brown, Langham and Company, Ltd., 1905.

The Edinburgh Review, CCCLII (1890), 310–316.

Elliott, G. R. "Browning's Whitmanism." *Sewanee Review,* XXXVII (1929), 164–171.

Elliott-Binns, L. E. *Religion in the Victorian Era.* London: Lutterworth Press, 1946.

Evans, B. Ifor. *Tradition and Romanticism.* New York: Longmans, Green and Company, Ltd., 1940.

Everett, Charles Carroll. "Tennyson and Browning as Spiritual Forces." *Essays Theological and Literary.* Boston: Houghton Mifflin Company, 1901.

———. "The Philosophy of Browning." *Essays Theological and Literary.* Boston: Houghton Mifflin Company, 1901.

Fairchild, Hoxie N. "Browning the Simple-Hearted Casuist." *University of Toronto Quarterly,* XVIII (1949), 234–240.

———. "Browning's Heaven." *Review of Religion,* XIV (1949), 30–37.

———. "La Saisiaz and The Nineteenth Century." *Modern Philology,* XLVIII (1948), 104–111.

———. *Religious Trends in English Poetry,* IV (*1830–1880; Christianity and Romanticism in the Victorian Era*). New York: Columbia University Press, 1957.

Farrar, F. W. "The Significance of Browning's Message." *Review of Reviews,* XV (1897), 185–191.

Fields, Annie. *Authors and Friends.* Boston: Houghton Mifflin Company, 1924.

Figgis, Darrell. "On Not Seeing Swinburne." *London Mercury,* IV (1921), 254–258.

———. "Robert Browning's Vision." *Studies and Appreciations.* London: J. M. Dent and Sons, 1912.

Fletcher, Robert Huntington. *Tennyson and Browning: A Manual for College Classes and Other Students.* Cedar Rapids, Iowa: The Torch Press, 1913.

Foster, A. Austin. *The Message of Robert Browning.* New York: Hodder and Stoughton, 1912.

Fotheringham, James. *Studies of the Mind and Art of Robert Browning.* 3rd ed. London: Horace Marshall and Son, 1898.

Fruit, John Phelps. "Browning and Tennyson." *MLN,* V (1890), 138–142.

G., W. N. "Browning's Optimism, So-Called." *The Dial,* XVIII (1895), 290.

George, A. J. "The Optimism of Wordsworth and Browning, in Relation to Modern Philosophy." *Boston Browning Society Papers.* New York: The Macmillan Company, 1897.

Gingerich, Solomon F. *Wordsworth, Tennyson, and Browning: A Study in Human Freedom.* Ann Arbor: George Wahr, Publisher, 1911.

Greenslet, F. "New Lights on Browning." *The Atlantic Monthly,* XCII (1903), 418–423.

Greer, Louise. *Browning and America.* Chapel Hill: University of North Carolina Press, 1952.

Gribble, Francis. "Robert Browning: Born May 7, 1812." *The Nineteenth Century and After,* LXXI (1912), 976–979.

Grierson, H. J. C. *Lyrical Poetry from Blake to Hardy.* London: The Hogarth Press, 1928.

————, and J. C. Smith. "Robert Browning." *A Critical History of English Poetry.* London: Chatto and Windus, 1947.

Griffin, W. Hall, and Harry Christopher Minchin. *The Life of Robert Browning with Notices of His Writings, His Family and His Friends.* New York: The Macmillan Company, 1910.

Griggs, Edward Howard. *The Poetry and Philosophy of Browning.* New York: Orchard Hill Press, 1905.

Gunsaulus, Frank W. *The Higher Ministries of Recent English Poetry.* New York: Fleming H. Revell Company, 1907.

Guthrie, William Norman. "Browning and the Drama." *Addresses Commemorating the Birth of Robert Browning Delivered Before the New York Browning Society.* New York: n.p., 1912.

Hadley, Arthur Twining. *Some Influences in Modern Philosophic Thought.* New Haven: Yale University Press, 1912.

Hardie, John L. "Seeing Browning Plain." *The Spectator,* CLXXXIX (1952), 848.

Harrington, Vernon Charles. *Browning Studies.* Boston: Richard G. Badger, 1915.

Hearn, Lafcadio. *Appreciations of Poetry.* Selected and edited by John Erskine. London: William Heinemann, 1922.

————. "Philosophical Poems of the Victorian Age." *Interpretations of Literature.* John Erskine, ed. Vol. I. New York: Dodd, Mead and Company, 1916.

Heath-Stubbs, John. *The Darkling Plain.* London: Eyre and Spottiswoods, 1950.

Herford, C. H. *Robert Browning.* Edinburgh: William Blackwood and Sons, 1905.

Hermann, Edward A. G. *The Faith of Robert Browning.* Boston: Sherman, French and Company, 1916.

Hershey, Heloise Edwina. "Browning in America." *The New England Magazine,* N. S. I (1890), 542–545.

Hickey, Emily. "Browning Biography." *The Nineteenth Century and After,* LXVIII (1910), 1060–1075.

———. "Glorious Robert Browning." *The Nineteenth Century and After,* LXX (1911), 754–770.

Holmes, Stewart Walker. "Browning: Semantic Stutterer." *PMLA,* LX (1945), 231–255.

———. "Browning's *Sordello* and Jung: Browning's *Sordello* in the Light of Jung's Theory of Types." *PMLA,* LVI (1941), 758–796.

Hornbrooke, Francis B. *The Ring and the Book by Robert Browning: An Interpretation.* Boston: Little, Brown and Company, 1909.

Hutton, John A. *Guidance from Robert Browning in Matters of Faith.* Edinburgh and London: Oliphant, Anderson and Ferrier, 1903.

Hyde, William De Witt. *God's Education of Man.* Boston: Houghton Mifflin Company, 1899.

———. *The Art of Optimism as Taught by Robert Browning.* New York: Thomas Y. Crowell and Company, 1900.

Inge, William Ralph. *Christian Mysticism Considered in Eight Lectures Delivered Before the University of Oxford.* London: Methuen and Company, 1899.

———. *Studies of English Mystics.* London: John Murray, 1906.

Innes, A. Taylor. "La Saisiaz in 1895." *The Contemporary Review,* LXX (1896), 262–276.

Jacks, Lawrence P. *The Life and Letters of Stopford A. Brooke.* 2 vols. New York: Charles Scribner's Sons, 1917.

James, Henry. "Browning in Westminster Abbey." *Essays in London and Elsewhere.* London: James R. Osgood, McIlwaine and Company, 1893.

Johnson, E. D. H. "Browning." *The Alien Vision of Victorian Poetry.* Princeton: The Princeton University Press, 1952.

Jones, Henry. *Browning as a Philosophical and Religious Teacher.* Glasgow: James Maclehose and Sons, 1891.

———. *Idealism as a Practical Creed.* Glasgow: James Maclehose and Sons, 1910.

Jones, Jenkin Lloyd. "The Uncalculating Soul." *Boston Browning Society Papers.* New York: The Macmillan Company, 1897.

Jones, Rufus M. "Mysticism in Robert Browning." *The Biblical Review,* VIII (1923), 229–245.

Kelman, John. *Prophets of Yesterday and Their Message for To-Day.* Cambridge: Harvard University Press, 1924.

Kendall, Joshua. "Apparent Failure, in Reality, Ultimate and Substantial Triumph." *Boston Browning Society Papers.* New York: The Macmillan Company, 1897.

Kenmare, Dallas. *Ever a Fighter: A Modern Approach to the Work of Robert Browning.* London: James Barrie, 1952.

———. "Robert Browning." *The Contemporary Review,* CLXXXIV (1953), 355–359.

Ker, W. P. "Browning." *Essays and Studies by Members of the English Association,* I (1910), 70–84.

Kilby, Charles S. "Browning's Cristina." *The Explicator,* II (1943), 16.

Kirkconnell, Walter. "The *Epilogue* to *Dramatis Personae.*" *MLN,* XLI (1926), 213–219.

Knickerbocker, Kenneth L. "A Tentative Apology for Browning." *Tennessee Studies in Literature,* I (1956), 75–82.

———. "Robert Browning: A Modern Reappraisal." *Tennessee Studies in Literature,* IV (1959), 1–11.

———, ed. *The Selected Poetry of Robert Browning.* Modern Library Edition. New York: Random House, 1951.

Lang, Andrew. "Mr. Robert Browning." *The Contemporary Review,* LX (1891), 70–81.

———. "Victorian Literature." *Living Age,* CCXII (1897), 753–758.

Leake, Mrs. Percy. *The Ethics of Browning's Poems.* New York: M. F. Mansfield Company, 1901.

Leavens, Julia Pauline. "President's Welcome." *Addresses Com-*

memorating the Birth of Robert Browning Delivered Before the New York Browning Society. New York: n.p., 1912.

Leavis, F. R. New Bearings in English Poetry. London: Chatto and Windus, 1950.

Lewis, Naomi. "Books in General." The New Statesman and Nation, XLI (1951), 161–162.

Littell, P. "Books and Things." The New Republic, II (1915), 330.

Litzinger, Boyd. "Browning's 'The Statue and the Bust' Once More." Studies in Honor of John C. Hodges and Alwin Thaler. Knoxville, Tennessee: University of Tennessee Press, 1961.

————. Robert Browning and the Babylonian Woman. (Baylor Browning Interests, No. 19.) Waco, Texas: Baylor University, 1962.

Lockwood, Frank C. Robert Browning. New York: Eaton and Mains, 1906.

Longaker, Mark, and Edwin C. Bolles. Contemporary English Literature. New York: Appleton-Century-Crofts, 1953.

Loth, David. The Brownings: A Victorian Idyll. New York: Brentano's Publishers, 1929.

Lounsbury, Thomas R. The Early Literary Career of Robert Browning. New York: Charles Scribner's Sons, 1911.

Lubbock, Percy. "Robert Browning." The Quarterly Review, CCXVII (1912), 437–457.

Lucas, F. L. "Browning." Ten Victorian Poets. Cambridge: Cambridge University Press, 1940.

Mabie, Hamilton Wright. "Robert Browning." Essays in Literary Interpretation. New York: Dodd, Mead, and Company, 1892.

McAleer, Edward C., ed. Dearest Isa. Robert Browning's Letters to Isabella Blagden. Austin: University of Texas Press, 1951.

MacCarthy, Betty G. The Psychology of Genius: Studies in Browning. London: The London University Press, 1936.

McElroy, G. R. "And Which, But Who,—Browning's Obscurity." MLN, V (1890), 91.

Macy, John. "The Victorious Victorians." The Bookman, LXVII (1928), 542–547.

May, Burma. "Tennyson and Browning Compared." Methodist Quarterly Review, Series 3, XXXIV (1908), 261–273.

Megroz, R. L. Walter de la Mare: A Biographical and Critical Study. London: Hodder and Stoughton, Ltd., 1924.

Mellone, Sidney Herbert. *Leaders of Religious Thought in the Nineteenth Century.* Edinburgh: William Blackwood and Sons, 1902.

Merrill, William Pierson. *Faith and Sight.* New York: Charles Scribner's Sons, 1900.

Miller, Betty. *Elizabeth Barrett to Miss Mitford.* London: John Murray, 1954.

———. *Robert Browning: A Portrait.* London: Methuen and Company, 1952.

Mims, Edwin. *Great Writers as Interpreters of Religion.* Nashville: Abingdon-Cokesbury Press, 1945.

Mordell, Albert. *The Erotic Motive in Literature.* New York: Boni and Liveright, 1919.

More, Paul Elmer. "Why is Browning Popular?" *Shelburne Essays, Third Series.* New York: Putnam Company, 1905.

Morison, Jeanie. "Robert Browning and Elizabeth Barrett Browning." *Chambers's Cyclopaedia of English Literature.* David Patrick, ed. London: W. R. Chambers, Ltd., 1906. III, 549–567.

Moxom, Philip Stafford. *Two Masters: Browning and Turgenief.* Boston: Sherman, French and Company, 1912.

Mudge, James. "The Poetry, Personality, and Potency of Robert Browning." *Methodist Review,* CLII (1898), 643–657.

N&Q, CLXXXIV (1943), 151.

Naish, Ethel M. *Browning and Dogma.* London: George Bell and Sons, 1906.

Nettleship, John T. *Robert Browning: Essays and Thoughts.* 2nd ed. London: John Lasse, 1890.

Niven, Robert. "Browning's Obscurity." *The New England Magazine,* N. S. I (1890), 577–581.

Noble, James A. "The Poetry of Common Sense." *Macmillan's Magazine,* LXIV (1891), 431–438.

Oliphant, Margaret. *The Victorian Age of English Literature.* New York: Tait, Sons, and Company, 1892.

Organ, Troy. "Browning's Message for Dark Days." *College English,* V (1943), 13–18.

Orr, Mrs. Sutherland. *Life and Letters of Robert Browning.* 2 vols. Boston: Houghton Mifflin Company, 1892.

———. "The Religious Opinions of Robert Browning." *The Contemporary Review,* LX (1891), 876–891.

Osgood, Charles Grosvenor. *The Voice of England: A History of English Literature.* New York: Harper and Brothers, 1952.

Padelford, Frederick M. "Browning Out West." *Cornhill Magazine,* N.S. XXII (1907), 253–262.

Palmer, George Herbert. "Robert Browning." *Formative Types in English Poetry.* Boston: Houghton Mifflin Company, 1918.

Parrott, Thomas M., and Robert B. Martin. *A Companion to Victorian Literature.* New York: Charles Scribner's Sons, 1955.

Peyre, Henri. *Writers and Their Critics: A Study of Misunderstanding.* Ithaca: Cornell University Press, 1944.

Phelps, William Lyon. *As I Like It, Second Series.* New York: Charles Scribner's Sons, 1924.

————. *Robert Browning.* 2nd ed. Indianapolis: The Bobbs-Merrill Company, 1932.

————. *Robert Browning: How to Know Him.* Indianapolis: The Bobbs-Merrill Company, 1915.

Pigou, Arthur Cecil. *Robert Browning as a Religious Teacher.* London: C. J. Clay and Sons, 1901.

"The Poetry of Robert Browning." *The Academy,* LXXVIII (1910), 37–40.

Priestley, F. E. L. "A Reading of *La Saisiaz.*" *University of Toronto Quarterly,* XXV (1955), 47–59.

Raleigh, Walter. *On Writing and Writers.* Selected and edited by George Gordon. London: Edward Arnold and Company, 1926.

Randall, J. Herman. "Browning, the Influence." *Addresses Commemorating the Birth of Robert Browning Delivered Before the New York Browning Society.* New York: n.p., 1912.

Raymond, William O. "Browning and the Higher Criticism." *PMLA, XLIV* (1929), 590–621.

————. "Browning's Casuists." *SP,* XXXVII (1940), 641–666.

————. "Browning's Dark Mood: A Study of *Fifine at the Fair.*" *SP,* XXXI (1934), 578–599.

————. "Browning's Poetry Fifty Years After." *University of Toronto Quarterly,* IX (1940), 138–151.

————. "Browning's 'The Statue and the Bust.'" *University of Toronto Quarterly,* XXVIII (1959), 233–249.

————. "'The Jewelled Bow:' A Study in Browning's Imagery and Humanism." *PMLA, LXX* (1955), 115–131.

Read, Herbert. *Reason and Romanticism: Essays in Literary Criticism*. London: Faber and Owyer, 1926.

Reilly, Sister M. Paraclita, C. S. J. *Aubrey de Vere: Victorian Observer*. Lincoln: University of Nebraska Press, 1953.

Revell, William F. *Browning's Criticism of Life*. London: Swan Sonnenschein and Company, 1892.

Rice, Philip Blair. "The Philosopher as Poet and Critic." *The Philosophy of George Santayana*. Paul Arthur Schlipp, ed. ("The Library of Living Philosophers," II.) Evanston and Chicago: Northwestern University Press, 1940.

Ritchie, Anne Thackeray. *Records of Tennyson, Ruskin, and Browning*. London: Macmillan and Company, 1896.

"Robert Browning." *The Atlantic Monthly*, LXV (1890), 243–248.

"Robert Browning." *Living Age*, CLXXXVI (1890), 771–784.

"Robert Browning." *The Nation*, XLIX (1889), 492–494.

Robertson, John M. *Browning and Tennyson as Teachers: Two Studies*. London: A. and H. B. Bonner, 1903.

Routh, H. V. *Towards the Twentieth Century: Essays in the Spiritual History of the Nineteenth*. New York: The Macmillan Company, 1937.

Royce, Josiah. "Browning's Theism." *Boston Browning Society Papers*. New York: The Macmillan Company, 1897.

Russell, Frances Theresa. "Gold and Alloy." *SP*, XXI (1924), 467–479.

———. "One Word More." *The University of California Chronicle*, XXVIII (1926), 99–101.

———. *One Word More on Browning*. Stanford: Stanford University Press, 1927.

———. "The Pessimism of Robert Browning." *Sewanee Review*, XXXII (1924), 69–77.

Saintsbury, George. "Browning." *Corrected Impressions: Essays on Victorian Writers*. New York: Dodd, Mead, and Company, 1895.

———. *A History of Nineteenth Century Literature (1780–1895)*. New York: The Macmillan Company, 1896.

Santayana, George. "A General Confession." *The Philosophy of George Santayana*. Paul Arthur Schlipp, ed. ("The Library of Living Philosophers," II.) Evanston and Chicago: Northwestern University Press, 1940.

Santayana, George. "The Poetry of Barbarism." *Interpretations of Poetry and Religion.* New York: Charles Scribner's Sons, 1900.

Scott, Dixon. "The Homeliness of Robert Browning." *Men of Letters.* London: Hodder and Stoughton, 1916.

Scott, J. M. D. "The Philosophy of Robert Browning." *Philosopher,* X (1932), 82–92; 119–125.

Scudder, Horace E., ed. *The Complete Poetical Works of Robert Browning.* Boston: Houghton Mifflin Company, 1895.

Scudder, Vida D. *The Life of the Spirit in the Modern English Poets.* Boston: Houghton Mifflin Company, 1895.

Sharp, Amy. "Robert Browning." *Victorian Poets.* London: Methuen and Company, 1891.

Shaw, Albert. "Browning and the Larger Public." *Review of Reviews,* XV (1897), 184–185.

Shaw, J. E. "The 'Donna Angelicata' in *The Ring and the Book.*" *PMLA,* XLI (1926), 55–81.

Shepherd, H. E. "Robert Browning." *MLN,* V (1890), 33–36.

Sherwood, Margaret. *Undercurrents of Influence in English Romantic Poetry.* Cambridge: Harvard University Press, 1934.

Shorter, Clement K. "Victorian Literature." *The Bookman,* V (1897), 480–483.

Sim, Frances M. *Robert Browning: Poet and Philosopher, 1850–1889.* New York: D. Appleton and Company, 1924.

Skemp, A. R. *Robert Browning.* London: T. C. and E. C. Jack, 1916.

Slicer, Thomas R. "Browning's Personal Interests." *Addresses Commemorating the Birth of Robert Browning Delivered Before the New York Browning Society.* New York: n.p., 1912.

Smalley, Donald. *Browning's Essay on Chatterton.* Foreword by William Clyde DeVane. Cambridge: Harvard University Press, 1948.

————. "Browning's View of Fact in *The Ring and the Book.*" *VNL,* No. 16 (Fall, 1959), 1–9.

Smith, C. Willard. *Browning's Star-Imagery: The Study of a Detail in Poetic Design.* Princeton: Princeton University Press, 1941.

Smith, Louise Worthington. "Browning's Place in the Evolution of English Poetry." *Sewanee Review,* XI (1903), 444–451.

Somervell, D. C. *English Thought in the Nineteenth Century.* London: Methuen and Company, 1929.

Somervell, D. C. "The Reputation of Robert Browning." *Essays and Studies by Members of the English Association,* XV (1929), 122–138.

Spurgeon, Carolyn F. E. *Mysticism in English Literature.* Cambridge: The University Press, 1913.

Stead, F. Herbert. "Browning as a Poet of the Plain People." *Review of Reviews,* XV (1897), 191–192.

Stephen, Leslie. "Browning's Casuistry." *The Living Age,* CCXXXVI (1903), 257–271.

————. "Robert Browning." *The Encyclopaedia Britannica* (1910), IV, 670–674.

Stevenson, Lionel. *Darwin Among the Poets.* Chicago: The University of Chicago Press, 1932.

Strong, Augustus H. *The Great Poets and Their Theology.* Philadelphia: American Baptist Publishing Society, 1897.

Swanwick, Anna. *Poets the Interpreters of Their Age.* London: George Bell and Sons, 1892.

Symonds, John Addington. "A Comparison of Elizabethan with Victorian Poetry." *Fortnightly Review,* XLV (1889), 55–79.

Symons, Arthur. *An Introduction to the Study of Browning.* London: J. M. Dent and Sons, Ltd., 1906.

Thompson, Francis. *Literary Criticisms by Francis Thompson.* Terence L. Connolly, S. J., ed. New York: E. P. Dutton and Company, 1948.

Tillotson, Geoffrey. *Criticism and the Nineteenth Century.* London: The Athlone Press, 1951.

Tracy, C. R. "Browning's Heresies." *SP,* XXXIII (1936), 610–625.

Trent, William Peterfield. "Two Estimates of Browning." *Forum,* XXXV (1903), 294–303.

Tucker, William J. "The Mystic Note in English Verse." *The Catholic World,* CLXVII (1948), 420–427.

Van Dyke, Henry. "The Glory of the Imperfect: Robert Browning's Poetry." *Companionable Books.* New York: Charles Scribner's Sons, 1924.

Vincent, Leon. *A Few Words on Browning.* Philadelphia: Arnold and Company, 1895.

W. W. "Some Child-Critics of Browning." *Academy,* LI (1897), 573–574.

Walker, Hugh. *The Age of Tennyson.* London: George Bell and Sons, 1897.

Walker, Hugh. *The Greater Victorian Poets.* London: Swan Sonnenschein and Company, 1895.

————. *The Literature of the Victorian Era.* Cambridge: The Cambridge University Press, 1910.

Waugh, Arthur. *Robert Browning.* London: Kegan Paul, Trench, Trubner and Company, 1890.

Weatherford, W. D. *Fundamental Religious Principles in Browning's Poetry.* Nashville: Smith and Lamar, 1907.

Weaver, Bennett. "A Primer Study in Browning's Satire." *College English,* XIV (1952), 76–81.

Weber, Carl J. *Hardy of Wessex, His Life and Literary Career.* New York: Columbia University Press, 1940.

Wenger, C. N. *The Aesthetics of Robert Browning.* Ann Arbor: George Wahr, Publisher, 1924.

Whiting, Lilian. *The Brownings: Their Life and Art.* Boston: Little, Brown and Company, 1917.

Wicksteed, Philip H. "Robert Browning." *The Contemporary Review,* LXXXIII (1903), 86–99.

Willy, Margaret. *Life Was Their Cry.* London: Evans Brothers, Ltd., 1950.

Wilson, F. Mary. *A Primer on Browning.* London: Macmillan and Company, 1891.

Winchester, C. T. *An Old Castle and Other Essays.* New York: The Macmillan Company, 1922.

————. "Robert Browning." *Addresses Commemorating the Birth of Robert Browning Delivered Before the New York Browning Society.* New York: n.p., 1912.

Woodberry, George E. "Editor's Study." *Harper's New Monthly Magazine,* LXXXIII (1891), 800–805.

————. *Studies of a Litterateur.* New York: Harcourt, Brace and Company, 1921.

Wray, Martha Marverhea. "Browning's Attitude toward Catholicism." M. A. thesis. The University of Tennessee, 1950.

Wright, Merle St. Croix. "Browning's Relation to Immortality." *Addresses Commemorating the Birth of Robert Browning Delivered Before the New York Browning Society.* New York: n.p., 1912.

Zwager, Louise H. *The English Philosophic Lyric.* Purmerend: J. Musses, 1931.

INDEX